This sealed packet contains your
unique access code to take the

IncredibleParent Strengths Assessment.

The code inside this packet is valid for one use only.

Do not purchase this book to use the code
if this packet has been opened.

If you want to know the fastest way to improve your parenting skills, this is the book for you! As a principal and superintendent of elementary schools for 22 years, I worked with thousands of parents and children and read many books on parenting and child psychology, most offering a one-size-fits-all approach to parenting that may not fit your family dynamic. *Incredible Parent* helps you meet the unique needs of your own family.

—**Kelly Parks,** author of *Exploring My Strengths*

A refreshing book that lifts the lid on how each of us is individually designed to be a parent. It describes how to be an authentic parent, deepening the relationships with your children.

—**Richard Sterry,** founder of Releasing Strengths, United Kingdom

Nobody starts out incredible, and perfection is out of reach, but practice and progress are at your fingertips right now with this book.

—**Jon Vroman,** host of the *Front Row Dads* podcast and founder of FrontRowDads.com

Your time as a parent goes so fast. Make it fun, enjoyable, and rewarding. Learn all you can from others who have been there. Analyn and Brandon's strengths-based approach is one of my favorite resources.

—**Tony Grebmeier,** founder of ShipOffers and creator of the Be Fulfilled community and podcast

According to Analyn and Brandon, parenting is a sacred responsibility. Most of us discover after having kids that they do not come with a user's manual. This powerful book helps every parent to identify and develop their parenting strengths.

—**Rhonda Knight Boyle,** author of *Turning Talents into Strengths*

Incredible Parent will help you identify your unique talents and abilities to cultivate strong family engagement and authentic connection with your children.

—**Kim Muench**, Certified Parent Coach

Being an incredible parent is not a box to check, but rather a progressive way of life. *Incredible Parent* provides powerful insights, questions, and real tools that can help anyone on the parenting journey no matter how old or young their children.

—**Darren and Lisa Virassammy**, TEDx speaker and founders of Flip the Script Family

Analyn and Brandon are guiding you through the path to a strengths-based family life. Discover your Super Six parenting strengths and empower your parenting.

—**Guillaume Le Penher**, Gallup-Certified CliftonStrengths Coach and Certified Incredible Parent Master Coach, France

Incredible Parent provides guidance that builds our confidence and strengthens our bond with our children. It is a definite must-read, regardless of the age of your children.

—**Polly Tonti**, Certified Incredible Parent Master Coach

INCREDIBLE

parent

Analyn & Brandon Miller

HARVEST HOUSE PUBLISHERS
EUGENE, OREGON

Cover design by Bryce Williamson

Interior design by Chad Dougherty

Incredible Parent

Copyright © 2021 by Brandon Miller and Analyn Miller
Published by Harvest House Publishers
Eugene, Oregon 97408
www.harvesthousepublishers.com

ISBN 978-0-7369-8169-9 (hardcover)
ISBN 978-0-7369-8170-5 (eBook)

Library of Congress Cataloging-in-Publication Data

Names: Miller, Brandon, author. | Miller, Analyn, author.
Title: Incredible parent / Brandon and Analyn Miller.
Description: Eugene, Oregon : Harvest House Publishers, [2021] | Summary:
    How can you take the next step from good to incredible? By shifting your
    focus to what you do well as a parent instead of dwelling on your
    weaknesses. —Provided by publisher.
Identifiers: LCCN 2020027136 (print) | LCCN 2020027137 (ebook) | ISBN
    9780736981699 (trade paperback) | ISBN 9780736981705 (ebook)
Subjects: LCSH: Parenting—Religious aspects—Christianity.
Classification: LCC BV4529 .M5458 2021 (print) | LCC BV4529 (ebook) | DDC
    248.8/45—dc23
LC record available at https://lccn.loc.gov/2020027136
LC ebook record available at https://lccn.loc.gov/2020027137

Printed in the United States of America

20 21 22 23 24 25 26 27 28 / Bang-CD / 10 9 8 7 6 5 4 3 2 1

Contents

Foreword by Bolaji Oyejide 7

Your Incredible Role. 11

1. Strong Moms and Super Dads 17

2. Awaken to Areas of Strength. 27

3. Embrace Specific Strengths. 39

4. Get Beyond the Grind 49

5. Model Your Message. 61

IncredibleParent Strengths Assessment Guide 72

Advisor Strength. 80   Organizer Strength. 128

Defender Strength 88   Sensitivity Strength 136

Fortitude Strength 96   Stability Strength 144

Gracious Strength. 104   Tenderness Strength 152

Inspiration Strength 112   Trainer Strength 160

Objectivity Strength. 120   Zest Strength 168

Notes 175

Foreword

by Bolaji Oyejide

I t was the spring of 2019.

As the dad of two tweeners, I'd spent the previous ten years writing kid superhero books to help my sons, and kids everywhere, find their superpowers. To discover strength within their struggles. Fifty books, a TEDx talk, and an international school tour later, Brave Young Heroes was positively impacting hundreds of thousands of kids across the world.

And yet something was missing. All my material spoke directly to the kids. For years, parents had been asking me how they could incorporate into their own parenting the affirming messages in my fiction stories. So, having no experience whatsoever, I decided to organize the world's biggest virtual conference about Raising Resilient Kids. Because that is what one does. Bite off more than one can chew.

Cue my wife rolling her eyes at this. She says I have a bad habit of jumping into the deep end feet first once I get passionate about something. Without a lifejacket. Or even much swimming expertise. (She knows me so well!)

But let us pause for a second. This could not be a whole conference of me, myself, and I, waxing deep on parental pearls of wisdom. Parents were asking some tough questions, and I could not be expert of all things to all parents. On my best days, I could not even be all things parent-wise to my own kids! For example, I woefully lack attention to details when it comes to boring, "adulting" things like school paperwork, dental appointments, and such. (Thankfully, my wife is more than incredible at these things, among many others.)

I discovered "The Incredibles" (Analyn and Brandon) through their 2019 book *Play to Their Strengths*—a heartfelt love letter from the current versions of Brandon and Analyn, parents of seven wonderful kids, to the younger versions of themselves (parents of three kids at the tender age of 22). The book resonated on a core level with me. The overwhelm and inadequacy they felt as parents mirrored my childhood struggles to find my place in the world as a short and shy kid with crippling social anxiety. *Play to Their Strengths* was the playbook for parenting kids like me who felt "broken" because of the way the world judged them. It took me two decades to find my superpowers. By this point I was a parent and had channeled my lessons into kid superhero books—Brave Young Heroes.

The first conversation I had with Analyn and Brandon was like an inaugural meeting of the Justice League. There were other "Supers" out here; I was not the only one. Analyn and Brandon were the first authors to come aboard the Raising Resilient Kids Summit. Though we had over 40 world-renowned speakers, authors, and PhDs with tens of thousands of session views, their session remains one of the most popular.

Okay, so we have established that parents are cuckoo for

discovering their kids' strengths and playing to those. But there was more gold to be mined here. Parents clamored for more.

Where *Play to Their Strengths* helps us identify our kids' superpowers, *Incredible Parent* turns its sights squarely on us. After all, how effectively can we model kids playing to their strengths if we parents do not first play to ours?

Many of us grew up believing the myth that you can be anything you want to be as long as you are willing to work hard enough to get there. We convinced ourselves that we could be great parents, just like the Joneses, if only we tried harder, put in more hours, burned the candle at both ends. For example, I mastered neither car repairs, nor fishing, nor camping...and at times wondered whether my kids were being shortchanged. Your list probably differs, but you can undoubtedly relate to my frustration, guilt, and exhaustion.

Incredible Parent dismantles this myth brick-by-brick. Analyn and Brandon make the case for us finding lasting parental success by focusing on our strengths. This bears unpacking. Are the Millers suggesting that you can be a jerk and excuse yourself, saying, "That's just the way I am. I can't fix my flaws"?

Not at all. They coined the phrase, "Yes, I love you. And no, you cannot have everything you want, because I love you." Playing to our strengths as parents requires self-awareness that is possible only through intentional and persistent self-evaluation. Accepting weaknesses doesn't mean neglecting the love part. It also does not mean you can't bring others into your parental "super-team" to give your kids valuable lessons that you aren't equipped to teach.

Analyn and Brandon show how some parents manage to engage consistently. They identify the 12 parenting superpowers and explain why they matter. They empower you to overcome Impostor

Syndrome on your way to becoming incredible. In all these and more, Analyn and Brandon have created a parental blueprint that could be as monumental as Stephen Covey's 7 Habits.

There is a freedom that comes from being unburdened of the frustration, exhaustion, and guilt that can accompany modern parenting. Analyn and Brandon reveal the power of strength-based parenting: You do not have to be good at it all. But you shortchange yourself and your kids if you don't find your own special superpowers and become the best you can possibly be.

I am as excited as I have ever been after reading a book. After you get this, chances are that you will be too. Read the book. Take the assessment. Discover your parental superpowers.

Bringing your best self, your imperfect self, to bear is an act of courage and self-acceptance. And we are here to cheer you on. Let us get to work, you incredible parent, you. This is when the fun begins.

Bolaji Oyejide
Bestselling Author of Kid Superhero Books
2020 North Carolina Youth Soccer Coach of the Year
TEDx Speaker
Creator of BraveYoungHeroes.com

Your Incredible Role

You have what it takes to be an amazing parent! We believe this wholeheartedly, and we wrote this book to encourage a generation of parents. Perhaps you believe this too, and you picked up this book looking for tips to help you keep growing. Or maybe you've come to this book looking for significant guidance. You are struggling in your parental responsibilities, and you're feeling something between frustration and desperation.

We don't want to leave out the brand-new parents either! Is that you? The one who is open to taking in all the learning you can get your hands on?

Whatever phase of parenting you are in, this is the place for you. We have lived through all those experiences and have gathered wisdom, insight, and tools to share. We've also created a way to look at yourself and your child in a new, transformative light. We can't wait to share all this with you.

Throughout this book, we will use the term "parent" to describe the sacred responsibility one takes on when raising a child to be the best person they can possibly be. If you are the biological parent of your child, this book will resonate with you. If you have brought your child into your forever family through adoption, this book will speak to you. And if you are your child's caregiver, grandparent, legal guardian, or foster parent, this book will build you up and empower you too.

We are parents to seven children, three of whom are in their twenties, married, and growing their own families; four are at home in their teenage and early adolescent years. We also have four grandchildren, all under the age of four. We know a thing or two about striving to be the best parents to our brood. We decided over a decade ago to leave behind some myths about parenting and pursue a course that would bring us and our children greater fulfillment.

Our Story

By the time we were in our midtwenties, we were raising three school-aged kids and doing our best to be "good parents." The thought of being great parents—much less incredible parents—was *not* on our radar. Our daily scoreboard consisted of goals like these:

- Get the kids up, fed, dressed, and out the door in time for school.

- Make sure at least one of us shows up to activities and after-school pickup.

- Check that each child has completed their homework.

- Feed and bathe them, say our prayers, and get them to bed…and to sleep!

Seriously, this was our definition of a successful day. We thought we were superstars if the day didn't include missing an appointment or raising our voices to end a quarrel between siblings. Then during a challenging season of our parenting journey, we were faced with two questions that forced us to think differently about our experience and the experience of our family:

- How could we become better parents?
- Were we willing to do what it took to improve?

These questions were posed to us in a variety of ways and by several different people and sources. We kept coming back to the truth that we longed to be the best parents we could be and the reality that we didn't know how to get there.

The Way of Futility

By observing those around us, reading books, and consulting with families we viewed as successful, we thought the way to achieve this growth was to identify the areas in which we were failing, focus our energy and effort on making these areas stronger, and hope for improvement over time.

So we tried. We really tried to be better parents by following this path. We reasoned that if we studied our struggles and tried to be better (different) versions of ourselves, we would undoubtedly improve our parenting.

We committed to being more organized in our household. We committed to keeping our kids on a strict schedule. We committed to establishing chore charts, engaging kids in learning options and play activities, and focusing on family time. We committed to interacting with teachers and coaches.

Reads like a good list, right? There was only one problem: We were *never* going to experience success in each of these areas. It wasn't that we weren't getting any bits of wisdom from the people and resources we were accessing; it was that we were following a path that we could not sustain. It wasn't personalized, and it wasn't realistic. It was an exercise in futility for our family.

We had bought into a lie—two, actually: "You can be anything you want to be as long as you are willing to work hard enough to get there," and "Hard work solves all." We convinced ourselves that successful parenting was about overcoming our personal character flaws and areas of lack and then working even harder. These lies set us up for frustration, which we started to take out on each other when we experienced yet another round of failure.

Can you relate?

Waking Up to Personalized Parenting

Have you ever received some good parenting advice and taken it for a spin? Was the advice given to you ever preceded by the words "If I were you…" or "What we did was…"? That person's path to success worked for them. The reason it most likely worked was because it was a path or plan that fit who they were and was at the level of need or excellence at which they already functioned.

Not all the endeavors on our list of things to improve failed. We enjoyed some nice growth in certain aspects of our parenting. Yet with each passing week, we realized we were investing our precious energy into trying to improve or repair our areas of lack, sometimes to the detriment of our areas of strength. We were exhausted but kept reasoning that "this works for others, so we will make it work for us too!"

What we didn't yet realize was that we would become better parents once we started parenting as *us* and not as the parents we thought our children *needed* us to be. We didn't have the tools or confidence to lean into who we each were and build on that foundation together. No wonder we were overwhelmed. And to be frank, our children were suffering right along with us. They had to deal with our exhaustion, our impatience, and the multiple times we switched to a different tactic. The constant trial and error wasn't ideal for their development, and we could tell it was having an impact on our relationship with them.

Success Through Strengths

We came to understand that if we truly wanted to be great parents, we first had to own up to our areas of greatest strength and focus more on what we did well instead of lamenting the areas where we were not as strong. No more working against ourselves by not being ourselves. We learned through experience, and subsequently through science, that our greatest potential to sustained success was to follow our unique path to excellence.

At first, this was a humbling experience. Coming to terms with an area of weakness does not necessarily feel good. Letting go of striving to be a different version of ourselves took some grace. It also required faith in the new perspective we were embracing. In our journey, when we let go of unrealized expectations, the disappointment gave way to understanding, and this birthed a new confidence in each of us. We felt it at home, at work, in our marriage, and in our relationships with friends and family.

This confidence ushered in liberation and a newfound courage that helped us face our fears of inadequacy head-on. Why? Because on the other side of truth-telling is great freedom and empowerment.

To a certain extent, we both suffered from Imposter Syndrome—we operated with a nagging sense that we could never really be the parents or people we were either acting like or aspiring to be. We couldn't free ourselves of that burden until we embraced a strengths-based focus for ourselves and our family.

We are still on our parenting journey, learning how to be strengths-based parents and how to see new opportunities for growth all around us. We are thrilled to be a voice in the global strengths-based parenting movement, and we hope to inspire parents everywhere to embrace a new approach to raising their children.

Friend, we want you to experience the freedom and joy of parenting in your strengths. Your journey will look different from that of others, but that's the beauty of parenting as yourself and not as us or some expert or a family down the street: You will no longer feel you have to measure up to someone else's measuring stick.

If you're not experiencing joy in your parenting, then we encourage you to read on. If you feel as though you are working against yourself or your child more often than not, then this is a book filled with encouragement and possibility for you. There is hope for better days, and sometimes it only takes a spark of inspiration to get the wheels of innovation and change moving. We believe in you; we know you have powerful parenting strengths just waiting to be unlocked and engaged.

Read the first five chapters, and then settle in for a ride as we give you what you need to discover your strengths and to start parenting in them with full confidence and joy.

Can you imagine how you will feel when you embrace *your* parenting strengths and rest in the knowledge that you have what it takes to be a great parent? We can tell you, it feels amazing! Incredible even.

1

Strong Moms and Super Dads

As we've grown on this parenting journey, we've had the privilege of meeting some amazing moms and dads—though trust us, they didn't start out that way. All of these incredible parents have three things in common.

1. They play to their strengths.

These strong moms and super dads take the time to learn their parenting strengths, and with increased self-awareness, they overcome the challenge many parents face: comparing themselves to other parents. This challenge is not unique; it plagues many parents.

The good news is, as we embrace our strengths, we grow in confidence, competence, and creativity. We see more options when we face challenges, we have more energy to meet the demands of parenting, and we are inspired to stay the course, even when things get hard. We can't wait to tell you more about how to use this book to learn and apply your parenting strengths.

2. They stop being their worst critic.

Let's face it: If you've been a parent for one day, you've already learned you are going to make some mistakes. Add a few thousand more days, and you are looking at a heap of failure. News flash: It comes with the territory. Parenting is challenging and not a perfect science. Strong parents come to this realization and learn how to let go of the unrealistic expectations they set for themselves and embrace the journey and destination of being the best parents they can be. This requires learning and growing and a lot of grace.

As part of my business, I (Brandon) often speak to rooms filled with industry, nonprofit, and governmental leaders. Through these talks, the issue of self-judgment comes up often. Each time I ask how many of the leaders present would acknowledge that they are their own harshest critics, many hands go up. To this, I offer a solution: Resign your position as the strongest voice of criticism in your life. In fact, literally writing that letter of resignation might be a good thing to do right now.

Being hypercritical is different from being driven and self-motivated. Those last two are great qualities. However, when your inner voice shifts toward negativity and bullying, you are being hurt more than helped. As a qualifier to this plan, I remind these leaders of two realities: We are not objective, and there are other people who, unfortunately, will be critical of us.

When these leaders let go of self-criticism, they are more effective and lead with greater confidence. It's the same outcome for parents.

3. They don't quit.

No matter what, these strong moms and super dads stay the course and give their best to be their best. Incredible parents understand that when it comes to raising their kids, their job is to see it through—all the way. It's a life commitment. As long as they are still in the game, the game never ends. These parents lead the way, showing their incredible kids how to become amazing adults who will live full and fulfilled lives, well-equipped to be strong contributors in their households, communities, and societies.

We believe more parents want to be incredible! We wrote our first book, *Play to Their Strengths,* as a guide to point parents in the right direction: to see what is strong in their kids instead of what is wrong in them. We've written this second book to inspire each parent to be their best; we created it as a resource for you to find out what it means (and what it looks and feels like) to be a strong mom or super dad, to identify your unique parenting strengths, and to live out those strengths in specific, useful ways that are healthy and fruitful for you and your family.

Every Child Has Two Questions

We've come to understand that as complicated as parenting can seem at times, the shocking truth is that what kids want to know and be assured of is quite simple. Our kids want to know our answers to two questions—only two. Understanding these will help you employ your strengths with a deeper understanding that at any given moment, you are responding to one of these questions through your actions, words, and choices.

Do you love me?

Every child wants to know if their parent loves them. This seems straightforward enough. Most of us would respond, "Of course I do!" However, with introspection, we come to understand that though the answer to this question takes a moment to say, it takes a lifetime to live. You see, we are always answering this question for our kids whether we realize it or not. We answer through the words we say or don't say. We respond through displays of affection or lack thereof. We tell them yes or no through words of either affirmation, advice, and appreciation or criticism, correction, and critique.

And then there is the most easily measured indicator of love many of our kids will look for—time. One person quantified the time he had spent with his parents before leaving home to go to college and found that more than 90 percent of the total time he was likely to ever get to spend with them had already occurred. He was 34 years old.[1]

We've reverse engineered this person's findings—remember, this was one guy's calculation—and agree that a disproportionate percentage of the time we will ever spend with our kids will occur before they become adults. Why is this important? Because our kids are yearning to know we love them and we have a limited amount of time to show them that we do. They want to know we are interested and involved in their lives and personally vested in their success. They look to us to be their heroes, their champions, their caregivers, their leaders, their coaches, and their mentors. Filling all these roles will take time, and since this is the best investment you will ever make in this life, it is so worth giving your very best effort.

We often meet parents who excel at making sure, above all things, that their kids know they are loved, and they prove this to them by taking time to invest in their kids. Our friends Darren and Lisa are excellent examples of incredible parents. Lisa is a real estate agent and Darren is the cofounder and COO of a consulting firm. They have two children, and they partner in parenting to ensure their kids know they are deeply loved.

Darren's work requires him to travel. From the road, he makes a concerted effort to stay engaged with his kids by calling frequently to check in and by keeping up with their daily assignments and activities. Although her schedule can be quite full, Lisa is focused on making sure her kids are well tended to, even when Daddy is traveling. When the family is home together, Darren and Lisa plan special family outings and activities to enhance their children's learning and strengthen the bonds of their family unit. Darren is a student of martial arts, and as his kids reached an appropriate age to participate, he invited them to sign up for various classes. Each of the kids were eager to join their daddy, and together the family has bonded as Darren and the kids each take part in their chosen activities while Lisa uses her photography skills to chronical their progress for posterity.

Even with all this effort to stay connected with and invest time in their kids, both Darren and Lisa felt they needed to be even more attentive to their young family, so they made a change. After a family trip, they decided to relocate to a place that had fewer distractions. We remember listening to Darren and Lisa share the news of their move with a great sense of awe and respect. We wholeheartedly supported their decision to place the parenting of their children first, even if it might cost them some short-term opportunities. Quality time always comes from a quantity of time. That quantity might differ in our families, but it has to be a priority if our kids are going to hear, see, and feel our answer to the question "Do you love me?"

Will you let me do everything I want?

The second question every child wants answered by their parent—"Will you let me do everything I want?"—seems direct enough. The child has a want, and the parent is in position to provide the want, so the child expects the parent to hop to it and give the child what they want. From the moment our tiny bundle of joy expresses their most basic wants in the form of a loud cry, they will ask this question often.

How we answer question number two has a tremendous impact on how our kids understand the answer to question number one, "Do you love me?" Letting our kids have what they want when they want it has been called "permissive parenting." This parenting style values warmth in the relationship between parent and child without attending to the need for parental control. We have learned the hard way that not every want a child has is good for them at the time they make the request—and maybe not ever. We've learned the proper controls we need to put in place to provide our kids with safety, security, and strong support.

When we give in to a child's wants just to quiet them down or satisfy their desire, we are setting them up for a future letdown. The reality is, we cannot have everything we want just because we want it. Oh, we do know how draining it can be when a child keeps asking, asking, and asking for the same thing. It can seem almost more painful to not give in to their request, even when it is clearly not the best thing for them.

Hold strong, parents—but not too strong.

Some parents exert too much control in their kids' lives. We confess that for a long time, we did this very thing. This style of parenting is referred to as "authoritarian parenting," and it values high control but lacks in warmth. Some of us were raised by authoritarian parents ourselves, and so we simply repeat what we learned. This top-down, command-and-control style answers no to the second question clearly enough—but at what cost? Incredible parents who at one time leaned into authoritarian parenting can tell us, it took time and awareness to make sure they were also providing enough love and acceptance to balance the equation.

Some parents turn to harsh parenting after being "too soft" and feeling like they've been taken advantage of. Even so, this move toward more controlling parental behavior will have a long-term negative impact. Parenting expert Dr. Ryan Darby says it this way: "Authoritarian parents tend to be overly focused on rules and obedience. They are often stern and micro-manage their children's behaviors. Their relationship with their children tends to be cold and unresponsive to the child. The love and warmth that are expressed are implicitly conditional upon 'good' behavior."[2]

As our kids age, answering the second question becomes harder. Adolescents and teens push for their independence and autonomy. In some ways, these years resemble their toddler tantrum years—though hopefully with more maturity in terms of how they make their requests. During these intense seasons, when a child's expressed wants collide with a parent's will to measure and monitor what is best for them, some parents lose resolve and eventually succumb to a form of parenting known as "uninvolved." From this place, warmth and control are both lost.

An uninvolved parent sets their child up to face extra challenges as the child traverses increasingly weighty decisions without the interest and intervention of the person who should be most involved. Incredible parents recognize that path all too well, as many of us have been tempted to just give in to a child's wants and passively go about our business without too much care or interest in the outcome.

Our ability to lose ourselves within our connected world, where information and interaction with others is literally at our fingertips, can open the door inadvertently to uninvolved parenting. Maintaining a high level of interest and involvement requires tremendous resilience. But if we let our children do what they want to do and give them everything they want to have, we will set them up for deep disappointment in their adult lives.

Your Best Answer

We have found that the strongest parents learn and lean into a style that has both warmth and control. This style has been called "authoritative parenting" but could also be accurately described as "strengths-based parenting." When we made the shift to parenting our kids by focusing on their strengths and doing so with an awareness of our own strengths, we found it easier and much more fulfilling to exercise both warmth and control. We made it our goal to continually reinforce the love we have for our children while also establishing clear boundaries for them to follow.

Dr. Darby offers this perspective on authoritative parenting:

> Authoritative parents have clear rules and high expectations for their children. They hold their children responsible for their choices. And they are incredibly supportive. They are consistent with love and warmth. The results of this style of parenting are amazing. Studies have shown that children raised by authoritative parents are more likely to be successful on almost every metric. Authoritative parenting is associated with better academic outcomes, fewer risky or problem behaviors, more friends, better social relationships, higher self-esteem, better mental health, lower BMI, more resilience, and the list goes on and on. They are just happier,

healthier kids who turn into happier, more successful, and better-adjusted adults.[3]

The commitment to stay the parenting course in challenging times is embedded deep in the hearts of moms and dads. Support and strength always seem to come from a community. Strong moms and super dads are incredible together. We have found that like-minded parents (and this includes grandparents and other parenting or coparenting caregivers) seem to find one another and form bonds of trust and support on their incredible-parenting journeys. These cohorts form at the sidelines of soccer games, in lunchrooms at work, in small groups at church, in the stands of basketball games, during visiting time after PTA meetings and business networking groups, among mothers in preschool children's groups, and within many other intentional or unintentional gatherings where the subject of parenting comes up.

Incredible parents know this one thing, and they know it well: You cannot be a strong and successful parent by going it alone. You need a community in order to best answer the two basic questions your kids have every day and in every season, from childhood to young adulthood and on through adulthood!

Yes, I love you.

No, you cannot have everything you want—because I love you.

2

Awaken to Areas of Strength

Every person interviewed at Facebook is asked the same interview question: "On your very best day at work—the day you come home and think you have the best job in the world—what did you do that day?"[4]

The genius behind this question is that it gets to the core of the applicant's primary motivation as well as revealing their greatest strengths. When a candidate can articulate what makes them feel like they have the best job in the world, Facebook wisely positions them to do that work as a significant part of their daily job. Instead of hiring a person for their brilliance and then managing them to be a different version of themselves by fixating on their weaknesses, this company aims to hire and support employees who are engaged in their work from the start.

The key to being successful in any endeavor of life is to lean into who you already are. This requires that we let go of our notion that we can be anything we want to be as long as we work hard enough. Let's reframe the Facebook interview question:

On your best day of parenting—the day you think to yourself, "I love being a parent!"—what did you do that day?

Take a few minutes to think about this and then write down your answer. If you find it difficult to articulate, perhaps it's time to evaluate whether aspects of your parenting style aren't true to your strengths.

How to Be Engaged

In our rapidly changing culture, we need to know our strengths to understand where we fit in. Our kids need us to know who we are so they can follow our lead and learn from us in a way that resonates with them and helps them learn their own strengths.

Playing to your strengths in life requires self-awareness through self-evaluation. In fact, of the qualities listed as most essential to effective leadership, self-awareness tops most lists as the premium quality to pursue. There are myriad self-assessments on the market today. Many of them are effective and quite helpful to understand different aspects of our personalities and proclivities. To list a few, Gallup's CliftonStrengths, Values in Action (VIA), DiSC Profile, and Myers-Briggs Type Indicator (MBTI) are all excellent assessments.

We have created the IncredibleParent Strengths Assessment to refine and deepen your discovery of your parenting strengths. One goal of the assessment is to help you learn more about yourself and gain a new appreciation for different facets of your personality. Accepting our different traits allows us to become the best version of ourselves. As we grow in this acceptance, we also gain appreciation for the strengths of others and marvel at the brilliance we find in our partners.

Another way to think about this is to reflect on the level of engagement we bring into our parenting. According to Gallup, people who focus on their strengths are six times more likely to be engaged compared to their counterparts who choose to focus on their weaknesses.[5] This translates to parenting in the following ways:

Engaged parents...

- look forward to spending time with their kids
- have more positive than negative interactions with their kids
- treat their kids well
- talk about their kids in positive terms to their friends and other family members
- achieve more with their kids daily
- experience more memorable moments with their kids

Parenting from a strengths perspective opens the door for a greater parenting experience for parents and kids alike. Engaged parenting leads to a kid who has more confidence, direction, and hope.

Why wouldn't more parents want to lead their families from a strengths perspective and enjoy these outcomes? The reality is that most do not know what they are missing and are unaware of the amazing benefits of shifting to focus on strengths.

Tap Into Your Talents

Looking at your life through a lens that focuses on your strengths and living in them takes commitment and a willingness to pay attention. A way to start this adventure is to look for and tap into your talents. Talents are patterns of behavior. Our brains are pattern-producing organs, and the more we focus on certain thought patterns and behaviors, the more likely our brains are to reproduce them. Identifying these patterns is not difficult, but it does take intentional effort and energy. Very likely, you have untapped talents—patterns of behavior—already in place that could be accessed with some introspection and investigation. At the same time, you also do not have certain kinds of patterns, and we would refer to those as low-talent areas. In our effort to become incredible parents, we want to identify both areas.

We're often asked how a talent differs from a strength. Let's think of a strength as a super talent—one that has been increased and activated with continual effort and energy over time to the point that it nearly always produces the intended outcome. Focusing our efforts on areas of nontalent, hoping to turn them into strengths is a misuse of time and a recipe for burnout.

Your greatest passion and power are found in your strongest talents, as is the perseverance to stay engaged with these talents as you grow them into strengths. Incredible parents possess all three: passion, power, and perseverance. We define the Three P's this way:

- passion—exuberance and fervor toward an initiative
- power—the will and capacity to overcome obstacles and setbacks
- perseverance—the ability to stay committed to the course over the long haul

Tapping into our talent requires hard work. But so does fixing a weakness! The difference is progress. With true talent, you see measurable growth and sustained success. The results are not only greater expressions of your strengths but also increased portions of the Three P's: passion to become the best parent you can be, power to overcome the obstacles and setbacks you will face, and perseverance to stay the course over the long haul.

The most successful parents, those who enjoy being engaged and who see the fruit of their efforts in themselves and their children...

- start with their strengths
- invest energy and effort in their strengths
- multiply that investment by sticking with it over time
- see sustained success

This is the essence of an incredible parent. This parent chooses to move past their fixation on weakness and inadequacy so they can focus on this formula:

Natural Strength × (Effort + Energy) × Time = Sustained Success

Follow the Five E Clues to Your Strength

Know your strengths: This is a message we reinforce to every parent. We cannot grow in an area we do not know. First, we have to know what a strength is or looks like in our life. Consider these descriptions:

- Strengths are positive qualities that energize us and that we perform well and choose often.
- Strengths are qualities used in productive ways to contribute to our goals and development.
- Strengths are built over time through our innate abilities and dedicated efforts.
- Strengths are qualities recognized by others as

praiseworthy, and they contribute positively to the lives of others.

- Strengths are the things you do that make you feel strong.

The first four in that list are the definitions we used to create our assessment and list of strengths. The fifth one is a great way to gauge whether something you are doing is being done through a strength. You'll find that helpful along your journey.

Now we move forward to get more personal and specific. No one can tell you what makes you feel strong; only you can do that for yourself. That's why we have created five clues to signal which aspects of your parenting are your strengths. As you read through these Five E's and respond to the evaluation questions, consider which parenting activities personally match up with each one. Then, at the conclusion, make a list for yourself of the parenting activities you are currently doing that match up to all five.

1. Enthusiasm

You will look forward to certain parenting activities or tasks more than others and find yourself drawn to them. These are areas of enthusiasm. They are marked by a longing or yearning to return to them.

Evaluation questions: When you think about your parenting over the past month, which activities or actions were you eager to do? If time was not a factor, what would you spend the most time doing with your kids?

2. Ease

When something is easy for us, it seems to come to us naturally.

It is as though the steps required for the activity or task disappear, and we flow through it without giving it much thought or worry. We are able to glide without turbulence.

Evaluation questions: In the last week, when did you feel like parenting was easy for you? What were you doing? Can you think of a time when you felt like you were "flowing" as a parent?

3. Excellence

Notice which areas of parenting you do with standout ability. These are likely those that have received third-party validation. Another parent or a teacher or neighbor may have pointed them out as your strengths and abilities.

Evaluation questions: When was the last time someone made a positive comment about your parenting? Can you recall other times you have been validated for something you do as a parent? What would you consider to be your standout abilities as a parent?

4. Energy

There are some things we do as parents that take energy from us and some that give energy to us. A true strength always makes us feel strong instead of exhausted or depleted.

Evaluation questions: What recently completed parenting task left you energized? What activities bring you the greatest satisfaction as a parent? Can you recall a time when you were especially energized after a day of parenting? What did you do that day?

5. Enjoyment

When the going gets tough, our strengths keep us going. Grit is vital for successful parenting. When we enjoy something we do in our parenting role, we will press past opposition, pain, or distraction to keep going.

Evaluation questions: What do you enjoy doing so much as a parent that you will keep doing it even when you are sick, tired, or running up against challenges? When you last felt fueled by pleasure while parenting, what were you doing? What other parenting activities bring you joy?

We hope this book will inspire you to watch for the Five E's and engage the strengths they illuminate in your life and within your role as a parent. Start with a simple understanding of how you would answer the question "What makes you feel strong?"

Play to Your Strengths

Recently, a minister shared a story about a health challenge he faced. As a young dad working hard to succeed in his career in the ministry, he found himself suffering from signs of too much stress, including an eye twitch that was not only embarrassing but very distracting to others when he spoke in public.

During a conversation with friends and colleagues, he was asked what he might engage in for stress relief and personal refreshment. He thought about what had brought him that sense of release and joy in the past: the thrill of competing in basketball as a collegiate player.

As we listened to him share, he voiced what many parents sometimes think: As adults, we don't have the time to play. Thankfully for this dad, he took the advice of his friends and joined a weekly basketball league with some colleagues. This required him to guard his basketball time closely. He had to say no to several opportunities and other commitments in order to stay in this place of strength. After just one season of play, his physical symptoms of stress, including the eye twitch, went away. He was a happier person and found he had more energy for his professional and parenting life simply because he was making sure he attended to his own well-being by securing time to play to his strengths.

Playing to strengths is something we should do not only as parents but in every area of our lives. It is valuable to note and honor our hobbies and interests as well as the facets of our vocations or occupations that represent our core strengths.

We recommend that you walk through the Five E's once again. This time, reflect on both your personal life and your professional life. Take out a new piece of paper, your journal, or a notes app on your mobile device. Walk through each clue to your strengths and note the areas and activities in your personal and professional life where you have enthusiasm, experience ease, note standout ability and excellence, receive energy, and feel enjoyment.

Now, considering each of the Five E's for both categories, make a list of the activities that match up to all five. These activities could be characterized as personal areas of strength.

Strengths at Work

As stated previously, Gallup notes that people who focus on their strengths at work are six times more likely to be engaged in their jobs. Further, people who do so are three times more likely to report having an excellent quality of life (well-being). The Five E's are a very helpful way to assess our workplace strengths and to seek to align our job to our strengths. I (Brandon) also have a very useful, straightforward tool that I use with business leaders, decision makers, and corporate owners and managers to quickly sort the areas of their work into three categories: grind, greatness, and genius.

Take a sheet of paper and create three columns. At the top of the first column, write the heading "Grind." Beneath that, write all the things you do at work that do not match up to the Five E's. These are the tasks that are required of you but that do not match up to your strengths. For both Analyn and me, responding to emails is a definite grind. We can get the task done well enough, but given another option, we would most likely prefer to do something else.

For the next column, create the heading "Greatness." Under this heading list all the activities you do at work that match up to your Five E's. These are the things you do that make you feel strong and contribute the most to your workplace engagement and personal well-being.

The third category and heading, "Genius," leads you to identify the most exciting and engaging category of your workplace activities. In this column, write down the things you do at work that bring out your very best and truly represent your standout abilities over time and through sustained effort. What are you known for among your peers, leaders, stakeholders, customers, and even your family members? We like to think of our genius activities as our greatness activities refined and magnified over time.

Now consider the percentage of time you are spending weekly in each category—Grind, Greatness, and Genius. See if you can determine a simple two-number ratio. For example, let's say a person is spending roughly 50 percent of their time in their Grind zone, 40 percent in Greatness, and 10 percent in Genius. We would call this a 50:50 ratio. Half of their time is in their Grind and the other half is in what we call the Strengths Zone:

Greatness + Genius = Strengths Zone

If you can begin to decrease time in your Grind—and we'll explore some ways to achieve this later—a ratio to aim for is 30 percent Grind to 70 percent Strengths Zone. We have experienced first-hand how this ratio increases workplace engagement and our levels of well-being.

Mom on a Mission

Wendi Cross is a great example of a woman living in her Strengths Zone—personally, professionally, and as a parent. Wendi feels strong when she knows she is making a difference in the lives of others, starting with her children and extended family. Along with her husband, Rick, Wendi discovered a passion for making a difference in the lives of at-risk kids. This led them to adopt a 12-year-old child from Ethiopia. Then Wendi and Rick adopted a baby with neonatal abstinence syndrome due to drug exposure in vitro. Add in her four biological kids, and we can all agree that Wendi has a full life!

Something amazing happens when a parent plays to their strengths and aligns their life to their Five E's. Great amounts of energy reserves are accessed, and it seems from the outside looking in that the person is blessed with superhuman abilities.

Wendi is a humble, talented, and generous leader and the cofounder of X-Hope, a not-for-profit organization created to empower at-risk children by providing hope, love, education, and forever families. She is *enthusiastic* about getting others to join her on her mission, and this passion causes others to give their time and money to support her cause. Motivating people and communicating clearly come *easy* to Wendi. *Excellence* shines through the true test of success, sustainability: For over a decade, Wendi and her team have seen their mission increase in reach and impact. If Wendi was depleted by her efforts, she would no doubt have succumbed to burnout. However, Wendi derives great *energy* by serving with others. She finds great encouragement when her kids serve with her and in their own strengths. As she models a life lived in that Strengths Zone made up of her Greatness and Genius, she experiences *enjoyment* that maintains her momentum even when she faces obstacles.

Wendi is intentional in living, leading, and loving in her strengths. Wendi is indeed an incredible parent.

3

Embrace Specific Strengths

The Five E's are meant to provide us with clues to our strengths. Can you identify your strengths in your role as a parent? What are you doing that hits all Five E's? We believe every parent has unique, powerful parenting strengths, and these strengths hold the key to finding joy in parenting. With the help of our colleague Dr. Ryan Darby, we set out to discover a way to help parents unlock their potential though what we call the IncredibleParent Strengths Assessment. As a result of our efforts, we were able to identify 12 distinct parenting strengths:

Advisor	Inspiration	Stability
Defender	Objectivity	Tenderness
Fortitude	Organizer	Trainer
Gracious	Sensitivity	Zest

In the next section we provide you with a short description for each of the 12 IncredibleParent Strengths. As you read through it, we encourage you to take note of the aspects of each strength you connect with. It is likely you'll read a few that sound especially like you. We call these super strengths—or more specifically, your Super Six because that is usually how many each of us has.

The IncredibleParent Strengths Assessment Guide provides a full-scale discussion of each of the 12 strengths. At the back of this book, in a sealed packet, we provide a unique access code for you to take the online assessment and learn your parenting strengths. We encourage you to read the rest of the book before taking the assessment, but if you just can't wait, at least read through this section and gain an understanding of the 12 before jumping to the end to get your report.

All parents use all 12 strengths on some level. The Super Six are the ones that match up to your Five E's the strongest. If you find that you only relate to four or five, no problem; these are your strengths, and you can learn more about each one. As you go through this next section, underline or highlight the words or phrases that resonate with you the most.

IncredibleParent Strengths

Advisor

You are the parent who takes the long view. You have a wise and mature outlook on life, and this affects how you parent your children. You don't lose sight of the things that are most important for them and their well-being and are able to step back and see the broader picture. This helps you guide your children and gives you the patience to withstand momentary frustrations. You are the parent your kids come to for advice. You might counsel for immediate or long-term decisions. A parent strong in the Advisor strength is wise, discerning, trusted, respected, knowledgeable, and an excellent source of counsel. The world is a big place. Parents strong in the Advisor strength understand this reality and seek to keep their vision far-reaching and their ideas current. Parents with a mature Advisor strength are also humble. They know what they know and realize there's so much more they do not know. Thus parents with this strength are excellent at asking questions and comfortable with the unknown because they know the answer is out there, even if they need to seek the strength of another Advisor to find it.

Defender

You are the parent who defends the weak and looks out for the underdog. You treat all people equally and believe that everyone's rights are equally important. You raise your children to do the same. Wherever they are and whatever they do, you help them live by the principles of justice and equality: To give everyone a chance, never take advantage of others, never bully, and always treat everyone with fairness. With your Defender strength, you encourage your kids to stand up for what is right, and you will be by their side in solidarity if their cause is just and their actions are intended to help others who need to be heard or supported. A parent strong in the Defender strength is fair, evenhanded, deeply devoted to justice and equality, protective, excellent at clarifying expectations, good at setting up boundaries, and great at helping kids understand the causes and effects of their actions.

Fortitude

You are a parent who never gives up. You are willing to do whatever it takes to help, love, and raise your children right. It does not matter how late it is, how tired you are, how cranky they are; you always try to step up and do what is best for your children. While you do struggle and sometimes fail, you are always willing to get back up and try again. When your kids are challenging, it is your strength of Fortitude that steadies you to keep your eyes on the outcome instead of the momentary challenge. To you, the journey of parenting is a test of your willingness to persevere and demonstrate the resilience and grit you hope your kids will emulate. Parents strong in the Fortitude strength are hardworking, resilient, gritty, strong-willed, goal-driven, persevering, dependable, and always looking to challenge themselves and others; they are involved people who make a difference and strong finishers.

Gracious

You are the parent who brings peace to your home. Your motto is that it's best to forgive and forget and realize everyone makes mistakes, especially children. You are quick to forgive, show mercy, and accept apologies. You are always willing to let your child make a fresh start and try again. When others seek to punish, you forgive and extend love. With your Gracious strength, you parent with the perspective that it is good to acknowledge your own errors and failures and to subsequently apologize, especially to your kid. You want to receive and give second chances. Letting go of an offense is something you do well; letting anger linger is not something you endorse or practice. You believe in resolving frustration before the day's end. Parents strong in the Gracious strength are forgiving, compassionate, accepting of weaknesses and failings, and accepting of people for who they are rather than what they do. They give second chances instead of holding grudges.

Inspiration

You are the parent who always motivates your child to try their best. You derive great satisfaction from seeing your kid realize their talents, grow in confidence, and find the best ways to express their strengths. When your kids encounter challenges, you are in their corner, talking them through the situation and focusing their vision on the possibilities instead of the problems. You enjoy setting your kids up for success by defining goals in their lives that are challenging yet attainable. Parents strong in the Inspiration strength possess a high level of emotional intelligence. They recognize their own emotions and those of others and can discern different feelings and label them appropriately. These parents equally possess drive and ambition. They are goal-oriented and enjoy using their Inspiration strength to help others—namely, their children—reach their goals.

Objectivity

You are the parent who always thinks through your decisions before making a judgment. Rather than coming to conclusions based on your emotions, you try to identify the reasons for your choices and respond appropriately. When you make a decision regarding your child, you explore all the facts and try to be objective. You weigh the pros and cons and thoroughly think through your decisions. In the end, you make the right choices because you took the time to think through the consequences. As your child grows, they will seek your help, advice, or guidance with their problems because you are open-minded and will not judge them harshly or let your emotions get in the way. Parents strong in the Objectivity strength make reliable decisions, are confident in their choices, and are excellent at getting to the bottom line. They are respected and appreciated for the care and consideration they take when sharing their knowledge and opinions.

Organizer

You are the parent who establishes routine and structure for your kids. Whether you are organizing the car pool, setting the chores list for the household, or working with your kids to help them manage their time or money, you likely thrive in a well-organized home. Your kids know they can trust you, and you build on this trust with consistency and thoroughness. You are the parent who thrives on order and structure, and though you concede that your child may not have the same organizational needs you do, you see the positive impact of a well-organized home and so work diligently to keep your family on schedule, following the plans you have carefully devised. Parents strong in the Organizer strength can be clear and concise with their expectations for cleanliness in the home and adherence to organizational principles such as punctuality. They are excellent planners and naturally take the lead by establishing routine and structure. Organizer parents thrive in effective systems and excel at managing highly efficient household schedules.

Sensitivity

You are a parent who is responsive to the needs of your child and seem to know what they are feeling. You always parent with compassion, especially when your children endure difficult times. When your child is sad, you feel their pain and seek to alleviate the hurt with your words and actions. You do not mind rolling up your sleeves and wading into the messes your kids make. You want your child to know you are there for them and will always have their back, no matter what. You seem to "just know" when something is amiss with your kids or when they are in a great space. This strength provides you with opportunities to demonstrate your care and concern by spending quality time with your kids, getting to really know them and understand them. You take great pleasure in this, and to you, this is one of your primary functions as a parent. Parents strong in the Sensitivity strength empathize, show compassion, and have enhanced emotional awareness. They leverage their Sensitivity strength to build strong bonds of trust with their kids and serve as a primary advocate for them. These parents value the connection they have with their kids and enjoy being in close proximity and providing personal attention.

Stability

You are a parent who keeps the family calm and stable. You do not let the stress and difficulties of parenting show. You rarely get angry or frustrated, and in those rare times when you do, you effectively deal with your negative emotions. Your Stability strength brings balance and calmness to your home. No matter what stresses exist outside of the house, your kids know that because of you, their homelife has a sure foundation. You are not bothered by your kids' faults and failures; to you, these are part of the learning process. As your kids grow and mature, you continue to be fascinated by them and so can overcome the pull to frustration when your expectations are not met and your kids fall short. Parents strong in the Stability strength are not easily angered and do not often succumb to fear or anxiety. They are calm in life's storms and maintain composure when faced with difficult circumstances. Their homes are peaceful, their demeanor is steady, and they are the rock their families depend on.

Tenderness

You are the parent who always tries to do nice things for your child. You play with them, cheer them up when they are down, celebrate their victories, and get excited with them. You're the type of parent that is always trying to do the little things to make your children feel special and loved. Because of your constant thoughtfulness and kindness, your children will never doubt your love for them. You model kindness to your children by going out of your way to help others in need. You are never too busy to help a friend or neighbor or even a stranger. Your children see this and know you are never too busy to help them as well. You will drop what you are doing when they look to you for aid or assurance. Your Tenderness strength is reflected in your kindness and overt displays of love and affection. Parents strong in the Tenderness strength are never hesitant to show love to their kids and display it with practical acts of service and thoughtful gestures. They generally have warm personalities and enjoy serving their children above their own interests.

Trainer

You are the parent who brings order to your home by making sure you clearly define the expectations for your child. They trust you because they always know where they stand with you, as you display your feelings of approval or disapproval for their behavior. You expect compliance and look for commitment from your kids. Your Trainer strength establishes the rules and boundaries that are in place so that the members of your household are considerate toward one another. Your kid respects you and understands that your discipline is born of your deep love for them and your desire to see them succeed in life. Parents strong in the Trainer strength excel at establishing codes of behavior and making sure every member of the household knows what is expected of them. They are strong at providing explicit rules of engagement and incentives for adherence to the social expectations of the family.

Zest

You are the parent who lives for each new day with passion and enthusiasm. You derive energy from and give your best effort to parenting, which is one of the great joys of your life. Your child trusts you and knows you are engaged in their life, never content to sit on the sidelines. Because parenting energizes you, you are always looking ahead with great anticipation toward the future in store for your child. You enjoy each new adventure you partake in with your kid, and they love your Zest for life. You never give half-hearted effort to your parenting and continuously look to be the best parent you can be through continuous growth. To you, making a mistake is the highest form of learning. You don't linger long in disappointment or discouragement after a setback. You move forward with purpose, eager to see your child become all they were made to be. Parents strong in Zest are playful and fun and love to laugh. Zest parents enjoy life and delight in being a parent. The adventure of parenting is an opportunity to keep learning and growing and to experience life through the eyes of their children. They don't take themselves too seriously and, as such, are highly relatable. Parents strong in Zest are often friends with their adult kids.

Narrowing Down the Strengths

Now that you have read through the 12 strengths, which ones resonate with you the most? Refer back to the Five E's. Which are the strengths that...

- you want to make time for (*enthusiasm*),
- come most naturally to you (*ease*),
- you do with standout ability that has been validated by a third party (*excellence*),
- make you feel energized and give you strength (*energy*), and
- you will keep doing even when it gets difficult (*enjoyment*)?

These are likely your IncredibleParent Strengths! Go ahead and add this list of strengths to your journal or notes for when you reach the section of the book with thorough descriptions for each strength.

Now that we know our strengths, the next step is to evaluate the time you spend operating in your parenting strengths. Return to the Grind, Greatness, Genius exercise to determine the time you are spending in your parenting Grind as compared to your parenting Greatness + Genius.

In the IncredibleParent Strengths Assessment Guide, we'll explain more about your Super Six and your Supportive Six strengths.

4

Get Beyond the Grind

The three primary human-development institutions—our homes, schools, and workplaces—dedicate a disproportionate amount of resources toward fixing our flaws instead of building up our strengths. Most of us follow this same model when we evaluate our own success as parents. We check to see how we compare to some standard we have set for ourselves, usually modeled after another parent we admire, and then we establish a plan to try to meet it.

To illustrate this point, when you went through the list of parenting strengths in the last chapter, you may have focused more on the strengths that did not resonate with you more than those that did. This is called "negativity bias," and we all operate with it to a certain extent. Our homes, schools, and workplaces reinforce this perspective and instill in us the idea that we follow the path to success by fixing our weaknesses.

Although this approach seems sound on the surface, it is flawed. Our culture is convinced we can transform our weakest areas into strengths—if we just *work hard*, we can overcome anything. Our movies tell these stories, our legends lead with these messages, and our heroes to some degree personify this.

We love the underdog. Like them, we believe we can overcome anything and be anything we want to be. And to an extent, this might be true. But at what cost? We need to ask ourselves if we are just fixing or truly flourishing.

There are two kinds of weaknesses—which we call strength struggles or non-strengths—that we will address here. The first is a lack of strength and the second is the misuse of a strength. Where we lack strength, we can strive over time and reap a bit of progress, but when we run out of energy, the gains we accomplished diminish quickly. It can be disheartening. But the more debilitating area of weakness is the misuse of a strength. Once we have started leveraging a strength in an unhelpful way and built up some momentum, it's difficult to slow down and shift. These strength struggles take deliberate effort to change, but they can be altered using the same formula that created them.

Overcome a Non-strength

Ryan knows he's a good dad, and he has a great perspective to share with other parents: the power of accepting both your strengths and non-strengths. Embracing who he is, in truth and with an aspiration to be more of himself in all the best ways, allowed Ryan to lead his kids with confidence, creativity, and kindness. He came to terms with the fact that when it came to the Organizer strength, he was not the strongest. Getting his kids places on time consistently, following a structured schedule, or even organizing pickup times for extracurricular activities would never be the moments Ryan would shine.

There are four strategies he applies to reduce the time he spends in that Grind zone of weakness while still making sure his kids have structure in their lives and get to school on time. These strategies will help him just as they will help each of us reduce grind time and overcome the weaknesses that might otherwise wear us down and distract us.

1. Stop it.

If the lack of strength is in an area that is not necessary and won't be missed, let it go. For example, some parents thrive on being active in and present for their kids' school activities, signing up for every field trip and serving on the PTA and volunteering to lead the car pool. If you are this parent, keep up the good work! However, if you are not, and your kids don't miss you nor expect this from you, let it go.

2. Sub it out.

If the lack of strength is in a necessary area and needs to be addressed, consider whether someone in your network of family, friends, service providers, or vendors could step in and lend their strength. If something in your home needs to be repaired and you are not handy with tools, make a call and sub it out. Whether you employ the service of a licensed professional or buy dinner for a friend who can fix what's broken, you will have resolved the problem successfully.

3. Sync up.

Consider who could partner with you toward a solution. For example, if one parent does well teaching and tutoring while the other does well preparing lunches and organizing the family calendar, then let those roles become routine. You can also sync up with those outside the home. Find partners for car pool teams or childcare sharing. To a certain degree, we all sync up with the extended family members, caregivers, teachers, coaches, and professional service providers (physicians and counselors) in our child's life. See all your sync-up partners as extensions of your strengths; treat them with respect and offer regular appreciation.

4. Seek support.

In areas of necessary action or progress that are not your strengths, look for tools and technology to help you accomplish the task or meet the need. Many of us rely on phone applications to help us set goals, monitor our calendars, solve equations, research answers to medical questions, or wake us up to start the new day. When technology is kept in balance in our lives, it can assist us in our weaknesses or strengths.

Realigning our expectations will lead us to accept a non-strength and find ways to overcome that lack with the above strategies and others we might devise. Ryan's kids did not suffer under his lack. Instead, they thrived when he put effort and energy toward the areas of his strengths. He was able to usher in assistance from others and the use of technology to help him shore up his commitments and organizational needs. The relief Ryan described was inspiring. He was free to be passionate about loving on his kids, telling the best stories, listening to them share their own, and genuinely taking an active interest in modeling the incredible parenting he does.

Embracing who we are is a gift to our families. By flowing in our strengths, we help children flow in their areas of genius as well. Parenting from this perspective empowers us to stay committed to our role despite the challenges we will face as our kids mature and undergo different stages of development. We are emboldened to persevere through the challenging seasons and truly enjoy the best parts of being a parent.

Strength Struggles

Our strengths are incredible sources of energy. Much like the superheroes we watch in movies or read about in books, for every good hero using their superpower to help people, a villain is using their superpowers for selfish purposes. At their roots, our strengths have four primary aspects we need to watch out for.

1. Blind Spots

These gaps in our vision keep us from realizing the impact of our strengths on others. To overcome blind spots, we require assistance from others to help us see their negative impact. We need an open mind and a courageous heart to be able to hear about these gaps in our vision.

After you have completed the IncredibleParent Strengths Assessment, we would encourage you to show the list of strengths to your spouse and/or parenting partners. Take a close look at the strengths and struggles lists in the Assessment Guide and consider whether any of the struggles fall into your blind spot.

2. Biases

We all are predisposed to gravitate toward certain things we relate to and enjoy, and this means we also keep our distance or veer away from the things we don't connect with as easily. Biases can form through our upbringing and will present in behavior that sends a message showing our preference. For parents with multiple children, these biases are particularly important to clue into, since the perception of favoritism is hardwired into each child. When that is confirmed through their understanding of reality and their processing of your actions and words, it can cause emotional injury. Your challenge is to respond to the exposure of a bias with maturity and to address it with intentional remediation. Alleviating the concern requires persistent effort over time.

When you see your list of IncredibleParent Strengths, you will no doubt note your Super Six and Supportive Six strengths. We include action items to help you effectively use your strengths to be the best parent you can be. However, it's possible that action items for your strength may not match up to your child's strengths and their preferences. We call these contrarian strengths, and most parents will face these to a certain extent. For example, let's say you are strong in the Advisor strength and you enjoy teaching your children and using family gatherings to share advice or instruction. It's possible, especially with multiple children, that one will enjoy this experience while another will not. Be careful not to force your strength onto your kids or show preference for the child who seems to resonate naturally with your strength over the one who doesn't respond as strongly.

3. Brokenness

Painful occurrences make an impression on us. They can break our spirit, confidence, and ability to trust. Brokenness causes us to retreat toward self-defense and expresses itself in unreasonable responses to certain stimuli. Detecting and tending to brokenness in oneself requires a gentle approach. We usually have a good reason we are guarded, and our strengths can act as a shield to defend us from further injury.

A key to understanding the impact of our brokenness is to bear in mind that a "past" pain could be as recent as an event in the same week and can trigger us to take out our hurt or pain on a person who did not contribute to the offense or injury. Even those who have thick skin or have done work to deal with past pain need to watch out for the ways brokenness can manifest through or be guarded by their strengths. If we acknowledge our vulnerability, we recover with more ease. Whether the offense we perceive against us occurred at work or in our personal space, we must be quite intentional to not allow our reaction to it to seep into our parenting. Our advice is to work through brokenness as soon as it is detected and identify the root cause. This is vital to our success in parenting and the well-being of our children.

4. Bravado

This is the belief that our way is right. Some bravado is overt. Other forms are subtle and come in the form of passive-aggressive behavior, which at its core is still an overplay of one's strengths. Bravado is tough to admit to, especially when we're confronted by kids and teens who challenge us. Needing to prove you are right or not allowing yourself to be proven wrong, even when it is obvious you are, are warning signs. To overcome bravado, parents can learn to listen more, contemplate thoughtful responses, and carefully choose their words and actions.

As an executive coach, I (Brandon) have found bravado to be the most difficult strength struggle to coach a leader to let go of. Blind spots, biases, and brokenness are rarely intentional, whereas bravado has a more active force behind it. Only the leader or parent can change the behavior.

When coaching leaders, I describe two primary motivators for change. The first motivator is movement toward pleasure. This opens them up to acknowledging that things could be better if a change were made, and the corresponding benefit incentivizes them to endure the challenge of modifying their behavior.

The second motivator to change is pain. When the behavior of a leader is causing a problem, and the problem needs to be solved, the pain and risk of staying the same essentially exceed the pain to change. As parents, if we misuse or abuse our strengths, they will cause pain for us and our kids. If we knowingly continue to function like this, we will be responsible for the consequences we face.

Sadly, the strength struggle of bravado is common. We see this in parents who misuse their Trainer strength and raise their voices at their kids or in parents with the Sensitivity strength who let their kids get away with doing wrong to maintain their relationship. Knowing we are playing to bravado is the first step; choosing to change because it is best for our kids is the move incredible parents make.

When considering how to overcome the combined impact of these strength struggles, we can hold on to four powerful mindsets. Remember, each strength struggle requires us to be in community with others who can lend their strengths to help us gain perspective and acknowledge the things we need to overcome. These are the four mindsets:

1. Humility

Almost nothing is stronger than this virtue for keeping our strengths healthy and effective. It can be difficult to admit when we are wrong. True humility is found in those who have accepted the fact that to err is human and to accept responsibility for our actions is strength. You know you are in the zone when it isn't very comfortable—you often aren't when you are growing. Incredible parents understand we are always growing and learning.

2. Honesty

Honesty with oneself is one of the greatest assets of effective parents. As a part of an advanced leadership course we took together, we were assigned the book *Leadership and Self-Deception: Getting Out of the Box*. In the preface of the book, we were faced with the idea that self-deception impacts every part of our lives and "blinds us to the true cause of problems, and once blind, all of the 'solutions' we can think of will make matters worse."[6] We have learned and relearned that we must honestly approach each situation with a willingness to evaluate what we can do to solve the problem within ourselves before addressing the other person or people involved. This effort has had a tremendous impact on our relationship with our children and keeps us on the lookout for all the strength struggles.

3. Hustle

To stay ahead of our strength struggles, we need to be moving toward a destination, not simply treading water. To hustle is to move with intention toward an outcome, and it is the mindset we seek daily. This doesn't negate our strong belief that rest is vital for effective parenting. But even in our rest, we try to be purposeful. To hustle is to stay one step ahead of our natural proclivity to slip back into behaviors we have worked hard to overcome. We imagine the image of our weaknesses trailing behind us; without vigilance, it'll catch up and set us back. Perhaps you've worked hard to overcome a pattern of behavior but then, with a shift of focus for a season, you found yourself doing it all over again and had to start fresh. Hustle is a state of mind incredible parents understand well. We are always moving forward with hope and have come to expect ongoing progress toward our goal of being the best parents we can be.

4. Honor

The mindset of honor is vital to overcoming the misuse of our strengths. When we honor our strengths, we place a high value on them as assets we possess, and we protect these assets diligently. This then helps us value the strengths of others and hold them in high esteem for the contributions they make and as integral parts of our family. To honor others is to see the best in them and to practice magnanimity by being quick to forgive offenses and overlook faults.

• • •

Brian Sharp is a CEO and business executive. He is renowned for his work ethic and delights in being busy and productive. His strengths are obvious to anyone he works with: Putting in long hours is a badge of honor to Brian, and he can easily burn the midnight oil and get right back up the next day and go hard again.

During a conversation with Brian, he shared that he needed to reevaluate his work-life balance, or life integration. His challenge was how to win at both business and parenting without compromising. He shared that he was going a hundred miles an hour as an executive and a hundred miles an hour as a dad, and he was burning out. He was missing balance and not giving himself the ability to find it in his schedule, so he was maxing out on both sides with diminishing results. After further conversation, Brian and I (Brandon) concluded that like many successful professionals, he lived and died by his calendar. If it wasn't scheduled, it didn't exist. So we came up with a plan to apply his work approach to his family. To be as tenacious about family time as he was with work time. To prioritize *both*. And to honor the time he had with his kids and eliminate the guilt of trying to do both all the time at the highest level.

At first, applying his work approach to his family took some getting used to. But with practice and persistence, Brian began to see real progress and was encouraged by the results. In a follow-up conversation a couple years after the initial effort began, Brian was as strong as any dad we've ever met, living an integrated life with his work and family life in harmony.

Interestingly, as Brian was gaining ground in one area, he gained ground in another at the same time—his personal health. As he became more active with his kids, he also became more active in his health-and-wellness routine. As parents learn to play to their strengths and overcome non-strengths or strength struggles, those efforts often improve other areas of their lives too. Brian is an excellent example of someone who tapped into his values and strengths and, with some realignment, experienced the power of managing his efforts toward measurable progress. Brian is an incredible parent.

The goal for an incredible parent is progress, not perfection. Stay true to yourself and manage your efforts by taking on one challenge at a time.

5

Model Your Message

Jeff Bezos, founder of Amazon, says, "Your brand is what other people say about you when you're not in the room." We think this is a true statement, and as parents, we are challenged to think about our kids' perceptions about us while they are under our care and in our homes and when they've moved out on their own. We've given serious thought and consideration to this challenge and seek to take an active role in forming our brand identity for our kids.

We believe an important part of becoming and being an incredible parent, or any kind of leader, is being intentional about the reputation you are cultivating, living out, and confirming in every area of your life.

Followers want to get behind someone who inspires them. As parents, we hope our children will be inclined to follow our lead and listen to our guidance throughout their lifetimes. To be honest, this wasn't always our way. For the first decade or so of our parenting journey, we cared too much about others' perceptions of our parenting—which is to say, we thought a lot about what those outside of our home thought about us. Living this way is a no-win endeavor. It is impossible to live up to the moving target of what others think about you as a parent. Sure, there is some value to modeling a strong example to your sphere of influence outside of your home; however, we think this should begin *in* the home.

As we gave serious thought to our parenting brand from our kids' perspectives, we determined we first needed to be clear on what we wanted them to think about us and endeavored to become the people we desired to be. As we saw it, 80 percent of our brand should be who we already were—our values coupled with our strengths—and 20 percent should be who we aspired to be—areas where we could grow and mature. We felt if we could be clear on both accounts, we could articulate a clear message to our kids about who we believe we are with confidence and conviction and at the same time share our aspirational journey to becoming better versions of ourselves as their parents.

As a couple, we pinpointed the values that were important to us and prioritized modeling these values to our kids. We didn't want to leave room for ambiguity or interpretation. This is not easy to do with your kids because they see it all! Every time our value message was compromised, we had the responsibility to own up to the misalignment and acknowledge the need to shift our speech and behavior to reassert the value. By the way, that itself is one of our values—taking ownership of our words and deeds and being accountable for the way we live out our values in real-life interactions.

Knowing ourselves and being known by our kids was and is a powerful way to embed our parenting brand in their minds and hearts. Being true to our strengths and giving maximum effort to grow in our strengths is another value we cherish, and it also increases the likelihood of establishing a clear and compelling brand.

For me (Analyn), this means endeavoring to be the best "Mama Miller" to our children, our in-law kids, and our grandchildren. I am active and involved in the life of our family, and I enjoy having fun and facilitating gatherings that allow for joyful interactions and the consumption of good food. Additionally, I want my kids to see my strong work ethic, which is a strength I have in alignment with our values. I seek to demonstrate this in my real estate business and when managing the practical affairs of the home, including organization, meal preparation, and fiscal responsibility. Since faith is also a central tenet of our values, I model alignment with that in my care for others and my service and support for those who are less fortunate than we are. A practical way I accomplish this is by serving on a board of directors for a nonprofit organization, as well as by urging my business to adopt service projects in our community and inviting my kids to engage with me in these efforts. Being true to my values, and playing to my strengths, is the brand I hope my children see in me and speak of about me when I'm not in their presence.

Meeting Essential Needs

When we model our message as parents, we are meeting the needs of our children. As part of our process to create these resources, we thought about the essential needs every child has and how each of the IncredibleParent Strengths meets these needs. The five essential needs for kids are love, trust, structure, correction, and hope.

1. Love

Going back to the first questions our children have of us—"Do you love me?"—we see deeply embedded in their hearts and minds a need to know the answer to this question. Depending on our parenting strengths, we will each answer this question in a unique and specific way.

For example, parents strong in the Sensitivity strength will show love by having in-depth talks and spending quality time together with their kids, having a keen sense of knowing when to speak and when to listen to them, and outwardly displaying affection for them.

Compare this with how a parent strong in the Objectivity strength will show love: by displaying an emotionally safe response to the individual needs of each child, carefully considering their words before speaking, and remembering the details their children share with them. Each of the 12 strengths will help parents show love to their kids in unique ways. As you read through the inventory of strengths, consider the unique way you show love and embrace the best and highest use of your strengths to meet this core need of every child.

2. Trust

This essential need is certainly not unique to kids. When we adults consider the leaders we will follow in our lives, trust ranks as one of the most essential qualities we look for in others in the workplace. Our children also need to be able to trust us. They need to know we will be there for them and we have their backs. Each IncredibleParent Strength will meet the need of trust differently yet all in a similar vein.

For example, a parent strong in the Fortitude strength will meet the need of trust by being dependable (especially in difficult times), following through on commitments, and demonstrating an unwillingness to waver in their support for their child.

Compare this to a parent strong in the Gracious strength, who will build trust by expressing mercy and forgiveness quickly, not holding a grudge when their child has broken the rules, and always offering them a way back into good standing. Trust is essential for just about every kind of leadership. As we establish our parenting brand with our children, we are essentially building confidence within their hearts and minds as we prove again and again that they can trust us.

3. Structure

Every child needs structure—a need that is met in very different ways depending on the strengths of the parents. Parents strong in the Organizer strength establish structure by calendaring a precise home schedule, organizing the home to function at an optimal level, and clarifying household expectations and standards for cleanliness and order.

Compare this with the very different approach of the parent strong in the strength of Zest, who will establish structure by making daily routines fun, encourage their kids to help cocreate the culture of their home so that everyone buys into the structure, and set up rewards and celebrations for accomplishing tasks and weekly assignments. Though the different ways to establish structure can vary vastly, they provide the child with some predictability in their life, which is essential for establishing a safe and secure environment for them to thrive.

4. Correction

There is much to be said about the different perspectives for providing correction to our kids. This essential need is found in how we answer the second most pressing question we shared with you in chapter 1, "Will you let me do everything I want to do?" We contend that the reasonable answer to this question is a firm but loving no. Yet the ways we get through the day-to-day reality of providing correction are as unique as our strengths.

Consider a parent strong in the Trainer strength. This parent will provide correction by explaining their core values in a consistent manner to their kids so they cannot be misinterpreted or misunderstood, by vigorously enforcing consequences when expectations are unmet or values are not demonstrated, and by providing constructive feedback to teach their kids to make better choices.

Compare this to a parent strong in the Stability strength, who will provide correction by gently explaining the consequences for negative actions, sharing consistent and affirming words during discipline, and relating to their children's failings and disobedience by telling stories to connect with them.

Both approaches are sound and effective if practiced with consistency and intentionality. You can meet the need in the way best suited to your particular strengths. Knowing your parenting strengths and gaining awareness and appreciation for how you meet the needs of your children is essential for building a strong and lasting parenting brand.

5. Hope

We have found that every one of us feels the need to believe in and look for better days to come. Children naturally have a level of optimism and, like their parents, want to cheerfully expect things to generally improve with time. Parents provide their children with hope. In the good times, this often is associated with gratitude for what we have and displays of generosity toward others—almost a hedge against taking things for granted and becoming spoiled. In the difficult times, hope floats us through the turbulent waves of life. We need hope—the light at the end of the tunnel or the ray of sunshine behind the dark clouds.

Parents meet this need in extraordinarily different ways. For example, a parent strong in the Inspiration strength will meet the need of hope by teaching their children to be joyful even in difficult times, reminding them of past victories, calling out their kids' strengths, and telling them they have what it takes to be incredible.

Compare this approach to parents strong in the Advisor strength, who will give hope by presenting the path out of a difficult situation, seeking the answers to resolve a problem, and looking ahead and sharing positive possible outcomes.

Our strengths, aligned with our values, will enable us to meet our children's needs. How are you intentionally showing love, building trust, establishing structure, providing correction, and giving hope? We have great news: Each of our strengths can meet each of these core needs. You might feel more effective at meeting some and less so others, but keep in mind that you have what it takes to be an incredible parent for your kid.

Your parenting brand is in your control; leaving it to chance is not recommended. Consider the 80 percent you could live up to today. Being clear about your values and strengths is an excellent place to begin. Make a list of the values important to you and the ones you know you are living out. Then add the strengths you have as a parent to that list. Combine this solitary effort with a casual conversation with your spouse and child, asking them what strengths they see in you. Then consider the other 20 percent, the aspirational growth you would like to see in yourself as a parent. Taking all this into account, you have the makings of your parenting brand. This represents what you are saying—to your child and the world— about what matters most.

Bolaji Oyejide is an incredible parent who is modeling his

message in all that he does in the home and in the world. He is the creator of Brave Young Heroes, a series of 50 superhero books featuring diverse kids who find their inner strengths despite differences like anxiety, autism, dyslexia, obesity, shyness, OCD, and more. Bolaji developed the ability to tell stories that inspire kids with the message that despite their challenges, they have a hero within them. Here's how he explains it in in his own words:

> I grew up a painfully shy kid. I couldn't tell you why. I couldn't tell you how. All I knew was that I felt different. And I didn't know why. It was frustrating. I knew one day I would change the world. But the world wasn't interested in listening to a shy kid. I felt like I was stuck in the wrong story. I felt like I was broken. The craziest part? It took me well into my twenties, to realize I wasn't stuck in the wrong story. I was exactly who I needed to be. I was still that same shy kid. But I got more comfortable in my skin. Once that happened, I took control of writing my story. Performed in the 1996 Olympics Opening Ceremonies, performed in an MTV music video, married my college sweetheart, applied to work at Pixar 12 times (rejected 12 times). Produced my first animated short in response, wrote more than 50 superhero books for kids in response. Reached over 100,000 book readers.[7]

As a dad, Bolaji seeks to inspire his kids as their coach, mentor, leader, and source of humor and family bonding. He is committed to being the best dad he can be and takes his role as a parent very seriously. The message he shares with audiences all over the world—"I

see you. I believe in you. And one day, you will change the world!"—
is the same message he models at home with his family.[8]

Being an incredible parent means being intentional with our
kids; it means being involved with them in their activities and showing we are interested in them by staying present and aware of who
they are and how they are growing and changing. This starts within
each of us as parents. Manage your efforts and measure your progress; you will be delighted with the fruit of your labors, both in
yourself and within your family. Dive into the IncredibleParent
Strengths Assessment Guide so you can get to know yourself and
grow as the incredible parent you were created to be.

INCREDIBLE

parent

*Strengths
Assessment
Guide*

Through our speaking engagements with groups and our many one-on-one conversations with parents, we discovered that it's challenging for parents to find the right words to describe the characteristics that enable them to be successful. Our goal became clear: to provide parents with a language of strength to define what makes them feel strong in their parenting roles. So we partnered with Dr. Ryan Darby, an expert in strengths-based development and positive psychology, to consider the best pathway to help parents acknowledge and name their parenting genius and understand areas where they are not as strong and may need support. Our mission is to empower parents to be the best versions of themselves for their own personal benefit and that of their children.

We used these four key definitions or descriptions of a strength to guide our research and development:

1. Strengths are positive qualities that energize us and that we perform well and choose often.

2. Strengths are qualities used in productive ways to contribute to our goals and development.

3. Strengths are built over time through our innate abilities and dedicated efforts.

4. Strengths are qualities recognized by others as praiseworthy, and they contribute positively to the lives of others.

Based on this framework, we built the IncredibleParent Strengths Assessment through a comprehensive review of parenting strategies, tactics, and styles. We looked at 60 years of research on what parents do to be successful, examined which ways were personality-based, and then used data analysis to group these behaviors into parenting strengths. The most common of these are what we call the 12 IncredibleParent Strengths:

Advisor	Inspiration	Stability
Defender	Objectivity	Tenderness
Fortitude	Organizer	Trainer
Gracious	Sensitivity	Zest

When you take the assessment, you'll respond to a series of statements and indicate whether you strongly agree, are neutral, or strongly disagree with how each correlates to your experience parenting. Once you join with thousands of parents from all over the world in learning your strengths, you will know what strengths you can build on to increase your confidence, competence, and creativity.

Super Six

Every person who is in a parenting role will utilize all twelve strengths. We call the top six of your strengths profile your Super Six. These are the strengths you most likely use with enthusiasm, ease, excellence, energy, and enjoyment. They are the strengths that will make you feel the strongest and net the best outcomes when parenting kids at all stages and ages. When harnessed, understood, and developed, these go-to strengths can relieve stress, increase joy, instill confidence, and provide a pathway out of parenting comparison and compromise.

The Super Six also come with warning labels. Our greatest parenting strengths can also be our greatest weaknesses. Watch out for misuse or overuse of these strengths. Help your partner find their balance as you also pay attention to and create your own.

Knowledge of our strengths is power. We hope to provide you with tools you can use to discover, develop, and deploy your strengths. The discovery process begins with taking the Incredible-Parent Strengths Assessment and continues as you learn the depth and relevance of each of your strengths. We encourage you to read the full description for each of your Super Six strengths and spend a dedicated season of time learning how to develop and maximize those strengths. Taking the time to really dive into one strength a week for a six-week period is an excellent way to grow in your knowledge of each strength and deploy it and its benefits.

Follow these steps as you discover, develop, and deploy your Super Six strengths.

1. Learn your Super Six.

Become familiar with each strength. Gain enough knowledge to be adept at reciting your strength to your parenting partners and your children. Learning our Super Six is the first step to strength actualization and effectiveness.

2. Lean into your Super Six.

Post your Super Six where you will see them regularly. Seize the power of your Super Six without hesitation. Put in the work to maximize them and bring them into focus as you engage in parenting your kids.

3. Leverage your Super Six.

Deploy these strengths to influence others and to move toward positive outcomes. Practice them to the point they are automatic in their application.

4. Lead with your Super Six.

Be known for the expression of these strengths in your home, with your kids, at the ball field, during recitals, in parent-teacher conferences, and among your parenting partners. Leading with your strengths is the result of learning, leaning into, and leveraging your Super Six.

Supportive Six

We have yet to meet a parent who is strong in all twelve IncredibleParent Strengths. Thus the next tier of strengths for you to discover are your Supportive Six. There are three different ways these can be expressed.

First, some of your Supportive Six could be strengths still in development, meaning you could someday leverage them with enthusiasm, ease, excellence, energy, and enjoyment, but it will take intentional investment of your time and talents. Strengths still being developed have the potential to bring tremendous benefit to you and your family. But it will require hard work and consistent effort and energy to gain the most from the strength. Usually the need to develop a Supportive Six strength is born of necessity. It is possible to accelerate the development of your Supportive Six strengths as you encounter needs in your parenting role that require them.

The second kind of Supportive Six strengths are learned traits. These are aspects of your parenting personality that you need or needed, but they never matched up to a full expression of a strength. Simply put, you haven't enacted these aspects of parenting with enthusiasm, ease, excellence, energy, and enjoyment.

Take heart—we all have Supportive Six strengths we grind with. Remember the triple G's—Grind, Greatness, and Genius? The aspects of parenting that match up to the things we must do but do not necessarily enjoy doing are the Grind. Most of our learned parenting traits fall into this category, and the idea of a Supportive Six helps us know which strengths specifically match this description.

We might find it difficult at first to differentiate between the strengths in development and the learned traits we engage when we need them. The key difference is energy. Developed strengths begin to energize us as we see results, realize excellence, and push past obstacles to keep engaging despite internal or external resistance. Learned traits don't.

Finally, some of the strengths found in the Supportive Six are, by definition, weaknesses. As hard as we might try, we cannot move the needle past mediocre, and when we cease to apply pressure, it seems to go back to the starting line. It is important for us to recognize which of the Supportive Six reveal our weaknesses, as these present opportunities to engage our parenting partners to leverage their strengths to fill in our gaps. There is no shame in acknowledging an area of weakness; it can liberate others to be vulnerable with their own.

Make the Most of This Guide

For each of the twelve strengths, we provide a general strength description and learning sections focused on that strength, whether it's one of yours or your parenting partner's.

At Their Best: descriptions of the best and highest use of the strength

Motivators: core drivers that move the strength to action

Rewards: benefits and goals the strength will help one reach

Strengths: strengths produced with effective utilization of the parenting strength

Struggles: common difficulties or frustrations created by the misuse or overuse of the strength

Meet a Child's Five Essential Needs: how the strength serves the five core needs of your child

Parent Action Steps: nuts and bolts of how to apply the strength in real life

Parenting Young Children: ways the strength serves young children

Parenting Teens: how the strength helps you connect with teens or adolescents

Parenting Adults: ways the strength helps you encourage adult children

Partnering with Parenting Strengths: how to recognize this strength in your partner and team up in positive ways. Partners can include a spouse, coparents, stepparents, caregivers, teachers, coaches, grandparents, aunts and uncles, and so on.

Bring Out the Incredible in Your Partner: how to honor and maximize your partner's strength

Understand the Triggers for Your Partner: what might make your partner misuse or overuse the strength and how to encourage its healthy application

As you work your way through the learning sections for each of your and your partner's Super Six, you will learn how to effectively deploy them for optimal use. This requires intentionality and constant calibration. You must adjust and adapt to ensure effective parenting.

Our kids are watching us. Modeling confidence in our strengths and vulnerability where we are not strong is life-giving and grants them permission to be strong in their strengths and aware of their non-strengths. Remember that the Supportive Six are not the focal point of the assessment. The information is helpful, but we encourage you to withstand the temptation to try to bring up strengths from the bottom of your list as an act of responsible parenting. We truly believe the most responsible thing, the most impactful, the most important is to play to your Super Six strengths and make these the focus of your parenting development.

You have incredible-parent potential just waiting to be unlocked. Discover and explore your parenting strengths, and raise your kids with confidence!

Start Your Strengths-Based Life

1. Get your code. Open the sealed packet in the back of this book to receive your unique access code to the IncredibleParent Strengths Assessment.

2. Go to **www.incredible.family** to take the assessment. It takes about 15 minutes.

3. Discover your strengths. Receive your report, read it, and note your top six.

    Change your life for the better (and your kid's life!). Read the rest of this material and dig into the transformative strengths portion of this guide.

Advisor

Wise, Counsels, Purposed,
Inquires, Strategic,
Mastery, Understanding,
Listener, Guidance,
Meaning, Knowledge

ADVISOR STRENGTH

Your Advisor strength is the foundation of your parenting. You have a wise and mature outlook on life, and this affects how you parent. You don't lose sight of the things that are most important for them and their well-being and are able to step back and see the broader picture. This helps you guide your children and gives you the patience to withstand momentary frustrations. You use your strength to provide emotional stability to your home. When your children are struggling, which all children will do, your Advisor strength helps them find balance and perspective. You are the parent your kids come to for advice.

— Advisor Parents at Their Best —

A parent strong in the Advisor strength is wise, discerning, trusted, respected, knowledgeable, and an excellent source of counsel. They seek to keep their vision far-reaching and their ideas current. Parents with a mature Advisor strength are also humble. They know what they know and realize there's so much more they do not know. Thus parents with this strength are excellent at asking questions and comfortable with the unknown because they know the answer is out there, even if they need to seek the strength of another Advisor to find it.

▶ Advisor Motivators

meaning and mastery

▶ Advisor Rewards

competency, mastery, knowledge, relationships, purpose, connection

▶ Advisor Strengths

patience, understanding, maturity, counsel, wisdom

▶ Advisor Struggles

know-it-all attitude, "I know best" perspective, talking rather than listening

MEET A CHILD'S FIVE ESSENTIAL NEEDS WITH YOUR ADVISOR STRENGTH

▶ Show Love

Give advice freely and often.
Actively listen.
Be understanding in difficult situations.

▶ Establish Structure

Ask quality questions.
Establish clear expectations.
Provide authoritative direction with control measures.

▶ Give Hope

Present the path out of a difficult situation.
Seek the answers to resolve a problem.
Look ahead and share positive outcomes.

▶ Build Trust

Offer wise advice and counsel.
Share experiences from past failures.
Hold your child's shortcomings in confidence.

▶ Bring Correction

Evaluate levels of severity in situations and respond accordingly.
Explain the consequences for behavior and follow through.
Provide instruction in the form of a lecture or discussion.

— Advisor Parent Action Steps —

Teach your child what matters most. Even if your child has this gift, their young brain is not developed enough to fully use it. Neurologically they are wired to focus almost exclusively on the present moment. You have a natural gift for helping them realize life is more than this moment.

When your children are experiencing a challenge, listen carefully and appreciate their feelings and perspective. Your inclination is to give them the right answers, so hold back and guide them to discover those answers themselves. Ask great questions, truly listen to their answers, and shower them with understanding.

Slow things down. The life of the modern parent and modern child is too busy. Help your family live in and appreciate moments of connection and joy. When life starts to seem out of control, pause everything. Stop and savor.

Eat family dinner together and enjoy the opportunity for informal teaching and bonding. Your children might resist when you overtly try to teach them. However, children love to follow examples. Dinners together allow for discussions about daily life and for you to model for them how to live life right.

— Parenting Young Children —

Your strength shines through when you sit your child down to explain certain concepts or truths you feel they need to understand. This could involve providing academic support and tutoring. With your Advisor strength leading the way, your young children will grow to trust you as the go-to person in their life for guidance and direction.

— Parenting Teens —

If you are the parent of an adolescent or teen, your Advisor strength comes through when your child and their friends seek you out for advice for decisions in their lives. You enjoy providing this support, and you are careful to discern the right insight to give your kids at the right time. This is your wisdom standing out as a strength of your parenting.

— Parenting Adults —

Your Advisor strength has most likely matured to the point that you see yourself as a sounding board for your kid to share their challenges and transitory decisions. Advisors know when to listen, when to ask questions, and when to ask for permission to offer advice. You do this with ease and excellence, and your adult child enjoys your wise words as well as your sage silence.

— Partnering with an Advisor Parent —

Your partner is motivated by mastery, feeling like they are an expert. You can feed this motivation by asking them for advice and seeking their counsel before making big decisions. When using their strengths positively, they will reciprocate and counsel with you, and together you will make great parenting decisions.

An Advisor has an amazing ability to bring perspective to parenting. Their ability to focus on what matters most will help you raise your children with purpose and presence. You can and should tap into their wisdom and understanding to make great parenting decisions.

Your partner is inspired by finding the meaning in situations and in life. When your family is struggling, your Advisor partner may look for the purpose of the experience. This is the source of their resilience and can buoy your family in turn. Finding meaning in both positive and negative experiences encourages happiness and the ability to recover from trauma.

If your partner struggles to restrain their Advisor strength and talks too much, doesn't listen, or forgets to ask for your advice, your partnership may benefit from structured parenting conversations. Some parents benefit from weekly "Parenting Counsel" sessions, during which they take turns to speak and reflect back what the other parent has said.

— Bring Out the Incredible in Your Advisor Partner —

Ask your partner for their opinions on parenting decisions and discipline.

Set up regular "Parent Counsels" with each other in which you discuss your child, including their current physical, psychological, emotional, and physical health. Discuss the state of your relationships with your kid individually and as a partnership.

Give your partner plenty of opportunities to teach your children and share their perspective on life events. If your partner is not doing this naturally, then start family routines like dinner table talks that give your partner an opportunity to use their Advisor strength.

Express your appreciation for your partner's wisdom and insights. Give thank-you notes, kind words of gratitude, smiles, and eye contact. Let them know that you see the best in them.

— Understand the Triggers for Your Advisor Partner —

If your children are no longer listening, then either the relationship needs to be repaired or your partner is using their Advisor strength inappropriately. Either way, your partner needs to first focus on trying to understand your child's point of view.

Your partner will become frustrated that "no one is listening." This sentiment indicates that your partner's advice isn't resonating with you or family members. Counsel together about why this is occurring and how they can use their Advisor strength in a way that builds relationships.

Defender

Peace, Justice, Fairness,
Rules, Inclusive, Advocate,
Protects, Creates Safe
Places, Helps Others,
Equality

DEFENDER STRENGTH

You are the parent who defends the weak and looks out for the underdog. You treat all people equally and believe that everyone's rights are equally important. You raise your children to do the same. Wherever they are and whatever they do, you help them live by the principles of justice and equality: give everyone a chance, never take advantage of others, never bully, and always treat everyone with fairness. You live your life with fair-mindedness and expect your children to do the same. With your Defender strength, you encourage your kids to stand up for what is right, and you will be by their side in solidarity if their cause is just and their actions are intended to help others who need to be heard or supported. You stand for causes, both big and small. This strength helps you protect your children. You can create appropriate and consistent rules in your home and in your children's life. Your emphasis on integrity and honesty gives your children a strong moral foundation.

— Defender Parents at Their Best —

A parent strong in the Defender strength is fair, evenhanded, deeply devoted to justice and equality, protective, excellent at clarifying expectations, good at setting up boundaries, and good at helping kids understand the causes and effects of their actions.

▶ Defender Motivators

fairness and justice

▶ Defender Rewards

peace, harmony, equality, support for the outsider or disadvantaged

▶ Defender Strengths

righting wrongs, standing up for what's right, including everyone, giving equal opportunities

▶ Defender Struggles

unsure when to fight and when not to, overemphasis on rules, easily offended

MEET A CHILD'S FIVE ESSENTIAL NEEDS WITH YOUR DEFENDER STRENGTH

▶ Show Love

Share your strong belief in equality for all.
Protect your children against injustice.
Advocate for your child in all circumstances.

▶ Build Trust

Be fair to your children.
Step in to defend your kid when someone is mistreating them.
Provide a safe place at home for your child to express who they are as they grow and learn.

▶ Establish Structure

Explain rules and expectations for all.
Hold your child accountable when it comes to playing by the rules.
Cocreate specific boundaries with your child's input.

▶ Bring Correction

Apply discipline with a deep sense of fairness in every situation.
Share how actions impact others in a negative way.
Reinforce what is right, fair, and just.

▶ Give Hope

Lead the charge for showing love and acceptance to all equally.
Paint a picture of a world through the perspective of equality for all.
Promise (out loud) to always have your kids' backs.

— Defender Parent Action Steps —

Create safe places for your child and other children to play by encouraging fair play and inclusion. When children are left out, coach them back into the game. Be a peacemaker in your home and on the playground.

Teach your child to notice when other children are not being included, are being bullied, or are being taken advantage of. These are common issues on the playground. Discuss what to do when they see these behaviors and how to defend and advocate for others.

Coach your child on how to advocate for themselves. There will be times and places where they are not treated fairly. Help them learn appropriate ways to be counted and how to have their opinions and feelings heard.

Take advantage of chances to talk to your child about your Defender strength. Discuss the importance of fairness, justice, and equity. Motivate and inspire them to stand up for others and be a person who defends others, especially those that cannot protect themselves. You stand for causes, both big and small. This strength helps you protect your children and model protection and justice to them.

Establish expectations and rules within your home that emphasize the importance of honesty, integrity, and fairness. Help your child understand the reasons these rules exist. You can create appropriate and consistent rules and boundaries in your children's life. Your emphasis on integrity and honesty gives your children a strong moral foundation.

— Parenting Young Children —

Your Defender strength is evident as you establish rules for your child to follow at home, school, play, or in the presence of caregivers.

Your child learns quickly that you will not tolerate cheating, rule-breaking, or taking advantage of others. You review the rules for each situation and scenario with your child to ensure they understand the expectations. You are explicitly clear that you will not allow them to get ahead by taking shortcuts or taking advantage of others. You desire for them to be a model citizen and the kind of person who looks out for others.

— Parenting Teens —

If you are the parent of an adolescent or teen, your Defender strength shows up with increased intensity as you help your child traverse the challenges of middle school and high school. Because of their increased exposure to more influences, you impress on them what is at stake when breaking the rules and even the law. As your child enjoys more liberties, your Defender strength compels you to keep tabs on them and to provide examples of people who model a life of integrity and fairness and who make a significant impact on the world. You desire for your teen to be respected, so you explain and reinforce how their actions have consequences for themselves and others.

— Parenting Adults —

Your Defender strength leads when you share with your adult child the causes you care deeply about and they, in turn, share those they feel strongly about. You are most proud of your kid when they achieve success by following the right path and living a life of fairness and equality. Your child understands this well and may be inclined to share with you the journey and the result of their experiences. Your approval is vital to your child, and in your strength, you give recognition to them as they demonstrate the values you hold firm.

— Partnering with a Defender Parent —

Your Defender partner will always fight for what is right. That is an incredible strength for you to partner with in raising your family. Your Defender partner is focused on justice, fairness, and equality. When they are utilizing the strength, they will defend these principles with love, grit, and patience.

If your partner is struggling in the strength, they may be losing their temper quickly or taking offense easily. These struggles are likely due to them feeling like something is not fair or equitable. You may benefit from discussing what they perceive as unfair and coming up with strategies to appropriately deal with such situations.

There are few things more valuable than someone who is willing to fight for what is right and stand up for equality, fairness, and justice. Recognize that this is who you are parenting with—a real superhero in the making.

— Bring Out the Incredible in Your Defender Partner —

Counsel together on fair discipline. Agree on standards you can consistently enforce.

Praise your partner when they do something to create a better world.

Give your partner opportunities to share their moral compass with your family. For example, you could watch movies or read books together that reinforce the principles of fairness, equality, and justice and then give your partner an opportunity to discuss them.

— Understand the Triggers for Your Defender Partner —

Pay attention to inequities in your relationships. Make sure that you are not taking advantage of their love for you or for your kids. You may want to clarify expectations for roles and responsibilities in your relationship and in your home.

When your partner is upset about something, listen closely and try to understand their perspective without minimizing their view. They have an intuitive sense of fairness and may be seeing something that you are not.

Watch for inconsistency with your discipline. To your partner, consistency is fairness and inconsistency is a factor for frustration.

Fortitude

Strong, Achiever,
Goals, Solid, Resilient,
Accomplishments,
Persevering, Grit,
Hardworking, Moral

FORTITUDE STRENGTH

You are a parent who never gives up. You are willing to do whatever it takes to help, love, and raise your children right. It does not matter how late it is, how tired you are, how cranky they are; you always try to step up and do what is best for your children. You struggle and sometimes fail, but you are always willing to get back up and try again. When your kids are challenging, it is your strength of Fortitude that steadies you to keep your eyes on the outcome instead of the momentary challenge. To you, the journey of parenting is a test of your willingness to persevere and demonstrate the resilience and grit you hope your kids will emulate. Because of the foundation you've created for your children, they always know that you will do whatever it takes to raise them right.

— Fortitude Parents at Their Best —

Parents strong in the Fortitude strength are hardworking, resilient, gritty, strong-willed, goal-driven, persevering, dependable, and always looking to challenge themselves and others; they are involved people who make a difference and strong finishers.

▶ Fortitude Motivators

goal achievement and morality

▶ Fortitude Rewards

accomplishment, closure, finishing, right action

▶ Fortitude Strengths

grit, sticking to what is right, seeing something through to the end

▶ Fortitude Struggles

stubbornness, inability to flex and bend, inability to quit

MEET A CHILD'S FIVE ESSENTIAL NEEDS WITH YOUR FORTITUDE STRENGTH

▶ Show Love

Believe in your child with great exuberance.
Patiently endure faults and failures.
Handle difficult seasons with a positive attitude and without complaining.
Keep a positive attitude in the midst of ease or difficulty.

▶ Build Trust

Be dependable, especially in difficult times.
Follow through on commitments.
Demonstrate an unwillingness to waver in support of your child.
Point to the positive benefits of resilience and call for courageous character.

▶ Establish Structure

Consistently adhere to the rules of the home.
Set an expectation for your child to finish what they start.

▶ Bring Correction

Challenge choices and actions that are out of line with established rules.
Reestablish standards for attitude and behavior.

▶ Give Hope

Express the belief that your child can overcome challenges.
Instill confidence by pointing out the strengths of your kid.
Remind your child you are "in this together."

—— Fortitude Parent Action Steps ——

Set some goals for yourself and for your family. What do you want your family to look like? What habits do you and your child need to develop? You may want to include the whole family in this goal-setting process. Once you and the family decide on your goals and habits, use your Fortitude strength to help everyone follow through.

Take care of yourself. You are a finisher and will often exhaust yourself to accomplish everything on your plate. Your emotional, physical, and mental health may fall by the wayside. If you are going to be at your best, you must take care of yourself. Sleep, exercise, and personal time are all critical parenting habits.

Simplify. Decide what really matters in your life and in your child's life. Then focus on those things. Use your Fortitude strength to hold firm to those things. Let go of the things that unnecessarily complicate life. They will take care of themselves—or they won't. But that's okay. They weren't important anyway.

—— Parenting Young Children ——

You demonstrate your strength of Fortitude when your young child sees your good example of hard work and your ability to overcome. You encourage them to see the obstacles and difficulties in their lives as opportunities to grow in grit. You urge them to press through challenges with a good attitude, overcome persistent problems, and finish what they start, such as team sports or school projects. Practically, you demonstrate your Fortitude strength by winning the battle of wills with your young child. They will recognize your Fortitude strength and come to rely on it in their most difficult times, when quitting seems like the best option.

— Parenting Teens —

When parenting an adolescent or teen, your Fortitude strength allows you to establish goals with your kid and for yourself at the same time. To your way of thinking, living the example of Fortitude is far more potent than merely telling your kid to practice resilience. As a result, you will establish goals that you will work on together as well as individually. You desire for them to learn to be people with grit, so it is essential to you that your kids see you persevering through trials on the way to your goal. Your Fortitude strength helps you consistently guide your teen's behavior. As your teen expresses independence and autonomy, you watch for ways to steer them down the right path and stay the course for the goals they have set for their future.

— Parenting Adults —

If you are the parent of an adult, you have become a shining example of grit and resilience for your child to depend on. When the going gets tough, and your child needs to depend on someone, you can be that rock. You relish this role and seeing them walk in some semblance of the resilience you sought to instill in them from a young age. You are delighted when your adult child is regarded as a difference-maker and strong finisher.

— Partnering with a Fortitude Parent —

Your partner will go the extra mile to accomplish what is important to them. You can rely on their grit and determination when life and parenting become exhausting—as they often do! They can be your strength and your engine to keep going and to do what is best for your children.

One of the reasons that your partner has such internal strength is that they see a clear line between right and wrong. They may see the world as black and white, right and wrong. When they have committed to a path, that decision becomes right, and failing to live up to it is now wrong. This makes them extremely resilient, determined, and sometimes stubborn. When your partner is in the strength of Fortitude, they will wisely choose which battles to fight. They will work with you and your children to determine what is right and to pick a course of action.

When your partner is struggling in the strength, they might become inflexible and stubbornly insist on outcomes they deem necessary, even if you or your child disagree. It helps to understand they are likely viewing the issue as a moral issue. It is right to act one way and wrong, almost immoral, to act another. In this situation, it's important that you counsel together and try to understand each other's perspective. Understanding, empathy, and compassion will do far more than arguing, fighting, and forcing your will.

— Bring Out the Incredible in Your Fortitude Partner —

When you start to struggle with parenting, ask your partner for a pep talk. Tell them that you need to rely on their Fortitude and watch them pull you up by the bootstraps.

Notice and appreciate the extra effort they put into things. Admire their strength and let them know that you see it, love it, and love them for it.

Support them when they lean into their Fortitude strength, even if you are exhausted or you don't think it is as important as they do. Your support is a show of love that they won't forget.

— Understand the Triggers for Your Fortitude Partner —

Your partner doesn't *want* to be considered the "bad cop," but they are willing to sacrifice and do those hard things. That doesn't mean that they should be the only one.

Take your frustration with their stubbornness and replace it with fascination. Ask yourself, "Why is this so important to them?" Lead with empathy and never belittle the things that are important to them.

Follow through on your commitments to your partner. They find closure and finishing tasks to be very rewarding. When things are left undone, it is like an itch that they can't scratch. It can quickly go from annoying, to frustrating, to enraging.

Gracious

Forgiving, Restores, Sees
Potential, Empathy, Love,
Harmony, Generous,
Welcoming, Encouraging,
Reconciliation

GRACIOUS STRENGTH

You are the parent who brings peace to your home. You live by the motto that it is best to forgive and forget and understand that everyone makes mistakes, especially children. You are quick to forgive, show mercy, and accept apologies. You are always willing to let your child make a fresh start and try again. When others might seek to punish, you forgive and extend love. With your Gracious strength, you acknowledge when you make an error or fail and subsequently apologize, especially to your kid. You want to receive second chances, so you freely give them. Letting go of an offense is something you do well; letting anger linger is not something you endorse or practice.

— Gracious Parents at Their Best —

Parents strong in the Gracious strength are forgiving, compassionate, accepting of weaknesses and failings, and accepting of people for who they are rather than what they do. They give second chances and don't hold grudges.

▶ **Gracious Motivators**

harmony and love

▶ **Gracious Rewards**

positive emotions, growth, harmony, reconciliation, lack of conflict, connection

▶ Gracious Strengths

accepting people as they are, seeing potential in people, forgiving and forgetting, not stereotyping, letting things go

▶ Gracious Struggles

avoiding holding others accountable, overemphasis on harmony, avoiding conflict and arguments, letting problems build up, mistaking disagreements for conflict

MEET A CHILD'S FIVE ESSENTIAL NEEDS WITH YOUR GRACIOUS STRENGTH

▶ Show Love

Display unconditional love and joy despite your child's mistakes. Quickly restore a relationship after a wrong turn. Generously provide for your child's needs and wants.

▶ Build Trust

Express mercy and forgiveness quickly. Don't hold a grudge when your child has broken the rules. Offer a way back to good standing for your kid.

▶ Establish Structure

Lead the way in seeing the best in all people. Gently instruct your kid regarding rules and expectations. Kindly remind your children of the consequences of their actions.

▶ Bring Correction

Share the emotional implications of your child's actions. Allow your child to face the natural consequences of their actions. Tenderly explain how harmful behavior is not in line with family values.

▶ Give Hope

Teach your child there is potential for greater good and growth in all people. Instill in your child the belief that there is always a path to forgiveness. Consistently speak encouragement to your child.

— Gracious Parent Action Steps —

Help your child learn to make amends. Part of making mistakes is undoing the wrong that was caused. At times, an apology may be enough. Other times, more emotional work and perhaps restitution is required. Help your child develop the emotional courage to apologize and make amends.

Learn to balance consequences and forgiveness. All children need to know that their behaviors have effects. If they can learn this when they are young, it will save them from pain and heartache when they are older. Help your child understand the implications of their behavior and, at the same time, express your love and forgiveness for them.

Use your natural empathy to teach your child to have compassion and to help them see things from other people's points of view. You can teach your child to do this by asking questions such as, "How would you feel if someone did this to you? How do you think they felt? Why did they feel that way? What do you think would make them feel better?"

Do not excuse harmful behavior. Finding reasons to justify someone's poor behavior does not help your child. Your strength is at its best not when you overlook problem behaviors but when you address those behaviors with grace and help your children learn how to make amends and change for the better. Only when they take full responsibility for their actions can they live lives of happiness and success.

— Parenting Young Children —

Your Gracious strength is seen when you respond with understanding when your young child does something displeasing to you. You are not one to harbor a grudge, and thus your kid comes to expect a merciful response, even when they display poor behavior repeatedly.

You model your Gracious strength by extending the same advantage to others in your life. This attitude of forgiveness is demonstrated when driving or interacting with other friends and family members, or at the store or the various events you attend with your child. You hate for others to suffer. Your kids learn compassion through your Gracious strength and as you teach them about historical and current events and the needs of others.

— Parenting Teens —

Your Gracious strength is well regarded by your kid and a strength they look to when they inevitably let you down by failing to act in a manner consistent with the rules and values in your home. The hallmark of this strength comes when your teen comes to you with their struggles and shortcomings. You see this as an honor and feel energized when you can be a source of strength to your child even during their darkest hours and most profound challenges. To you, this is your opportunity to show them understanding, love, compassion, grace, mercy, forgiveness, and hope. It is also the time to help your teen learn and grow and mature.

— Parenting Adults —

If you are the parent of an adult child, your Gracious strength has likely ushered you to the position of trusted confidant for them. In the times of their greatest need and challenges as well as triumphs, you are the parent they wish to share with. You enjoy this role and hold their problems in the deepest of confidence. They know you as a forgiving person who can see a path through their challenges as well as navigate how to handle offenses from others. Your child knows you believe that to forgive and forget is far better and healthier than to hold grudges and live in anger. It is likely you are sought to lend your perspective and your Gracious strength to them in the difficult seasons of their lives.

— Partnering with a Gracious Parent —

Your partner is full of love, acceptance, and forgiveness. Your child will always feel like your partner is in their corner, no matter what they do. Every child needs unconditional love, and because of your Gracious partner, yours will always have it.

Your partner's Gracious strength comes from an intense need for harmony and love. When people fight or hold grudges, it can cause your partner deep pain. They hate to see anger, hurt, and conflict. When your partner is operating in the strength of Graciousness, they readily forgive and teach your child how to appropriately make amends when they make a mistake. This creates a home of peace and love.

When your partner is struggling with their Gracious strength, they can ignore or excuse poor behavior. To avoid conflict and anger, they might also be inconsistent in their discipline or not enforce boundaries. If this is the case, you and your partner may benefit from switching from punishment-based discipline (for example, time-outs or groundings for a set period of time) to repentance-based discipline (such as withholding privileges until amends are made or behavior is improved).

— Bring Out the Incredible in Your Gracious Partner —

Let your partner's Gracious strength temper your discipline. Work together—listening to each other—when setting consequences for inappropriate behavior.

Ask your partner to help you build better relationships with your children. Your partner can sense when things are amiss. They can help you repair a damaged relationship and prevent any cracks from spreading.

Use repentance-based discipline instead of punishment-based discipline.

— Understand the Triggers for Your Gracious Partner —

Try not to discipline your children in anger. This will cause your partner pain and may lead to resentment and conflict between the two of you. Discipline from a place of calm and love rather than anger and vengeance. You can do this by using gentle, criticism-free language.

How to approach discipline is a potential source of conflict between you and your Gracious partner. When you are quite stern, you will find yourself fighting both your child and your spouse. Avoid unduly harsh disciplinary actions.

Inspiration

Encourager, Dream,
Joyful, Motivational,
Achievement, Charisma,
Change, Storyteller,
Ambitious, Enthusiastic

INSPIRATION STRENGTH

You are the parent who always motivates your child to try their best. You derive great satisfaction from seeing your kid realize their talents, grow in confidence, and the best ways to express their strengths. When your kids encounter challenges, you are in their corner, talking them through the situation and focusing their vision on the possibilities instead of the problems. You enjoy setting your kids up for success by defining goals in their lives that are challenging yet attainable.

— Inspiration Parents at Their Best —

Parents strong in the Inspiration strength possess a high level of emotional intelligence. They recognize their own emotions and those of others and can discern different feelings and label them appropriately. These parents equally possess drive and ambition. They are goal-oriented and enjoy using their Inspiration strength to help others—namely, their children—reach their goals.

▶ **Inspiration Motivators**

ambition and achievement

▶ **Inspiration Strengths**

enthusiasm, drive, ambition, determination, charisma, emotional intelligence

▶ **Inspiration Rewards**

change, influence, connection, admiration, growth

▶ **Inspiration Struggles**

lack of follow-up, initial momentum but little follow-through, emotional decision-making

MEET A CHILD'S FIVE ESSENTIAL NEEDS WITH YOUR INSPIRATION STRENGTH

▶ **Show Love**

Display an enthusiastic outlook in all situations.
Call out the best parts of who your child is and who they can become.
Warmly display affection through words and touch.

▶ **Build Trust**

Express encouraging words that build up your child.
Show up to events and presentations.
Tell the truth to your child.

▶ **Establish Structure**

Set an example of how to live and act.
Clarify house and life rules.
Set goals and establish routines.

▶ **Bring Correction**

Share from your own experiences.
Give clearly defined consequences.
Express displeasure to your child and explain the consequences for decisions.

▶ **Give Hope**

Teach your child to be joyful even in difficult times.
Remind your kid of past victories.
Call out your kid's strengths and tell them they have what it takes to be incredible.

— Inspiration Parent Action Steps —

Inspire your child to achieve their goals. Have meaningful conversations with them about what they want from a school, sports, life, and so on. Discover what they truly want out of these things. Use your Inspiration strength to instill the confidence and motivation to pursue those goals.

Be careful not to encourage your goals for your child rather than their own. You are incredibly influential, and you might not notice when you push your hopes onto them. They are their own person and might have goals that are different from yours. And that's okay. They are not you. They are them. Use your Inspiration talent to help them be the people they want to be.

Collect stories and share them with your children. This is a great way to use your strength to teach them. Find parables and proverbs you can share with your children to motivate and inspire them.

Inspire, then support. You are fantastic at influencing your children. They will get motivated and excited after they talk to you. But then the hard work starts. The challenges will start coming. The frustrations will set in. Be there for them during those times too. Offer continued support and encouragement. Help them follow through.

— Parenting Young Children —

You may enjoy being a coach or teacher in extracurricular activities your young child engages in. This role, official or unofficial, lets you influence their mindset and teach them the grand perspective of being gritty—that is, to not give up even when things are tough. With your little one, you demonstrate a model of success by sharing the goals you set for yourself and the steps you take to reach those goals. Since younger kids look to their parents for inspiration, you take great pleasure in being the primary influencer in your child's life and making time to have "talks" with them about those things that inspire them. During this season of parenting, you should stay in constant discovery mode with your child so you can learn the ways to motivate them to be their best and do their best.

— Parenting Teens —

This season of your kid's life takes on some complexity regarding your position as the primary influencer. You want to remain in an essential role while also allowing your teen to learn to make choices and understand consequences. During these years, your strategy remains the same, yet your tactics take on a different form. The mentorship you provide your teen, along with your understanding of their strengths and weaknesses, makes you a trusted source for guidance and instruction. One of your roles is to give your teen hope by inspiring them to see the possibilities in front of them and to work diligently to reach their objectives. You may enjoy the opportunity to set goals with your teen and work with them to achieve those goals in areas such as fitness, finances, friendships, or learning. You might enjoy discovering a new hobby together or finding good deals when shopping.

— Parenting Adults —

Your strength of Inspiration will be a tremendous resource for your grown child as they navigate the stress and turmoil of adulthood. They will face constant challenges in school, on their career path, when dating, in married life, when raising their own kids, and so on.

At times when they are completely overwhelmed and need someone to motivate them, you will come through as a voice of inspiration, hope, and strength. You will help them see their own strength and fight their way through those difficult times. You will always be the voice, the support, and the loving presence that helps them reach new heights and live their best life.

— Partnering with an Inspiration Parent —

Your partner sees potential and dreams big for themselves, for you, and for your kids. They will lift, inspire, and motivate your children to be their best selves. They can see a bright future for all of you and can use their Inspiration strength to keep you motivated to achieve it.

Your partner is enthusiastic, idealistic, and full of passion. Deeply ambitious, your partner wants to do great things. When your partner is in the strength of Inspiration, they will help your child achieve their goals and aspirations.

If your partner is struggling in their Inspiration, they might push too hard and create resentment. If that is the case, you can bring out the best in your partner by helping them inspire with love, compassion, and unconditional acceptance. Help them remember that your child first and foremost needs to know that each parent cares.

— Bring Out the Incredible in Your Inspiration Partner —

Enroll your kids into an activity that your partner can get excited about. Let your partner take ownership of mentoring and guiding them in these activities. Only step in if (maybe when) your partner gets too serious about it.

Set dream goals as a family. Your partner will get excited to see the future of what could be. Make a vision board, put it where everyone can see it, and talk about it often.

Support your partner's dreams by listening to and admiring their vision. Express your love and support often.

— Understand the Triggers for Your Inspiration Partner —

Avoid naysaying their goals. Your partner dreams big; some of their dreams are unrealistic. They will figure that out. You don't need to be the one who always pops their bubble.

Never shame your partner for failing. Life is full of mistakes and unrealized goals. Your partner will fail—and possibly fail a lot! They will be hard enough on themselves for failing. You just need to love them through it with compassion and encouragement.

Notice when your partner stops dreaming. Dreaming is part of who they are. When they stop dreaming, something is wrong.

Objectivity

Good Decision-Making,
Weighs Risk, Analytical,
Reasoning, Calm,
Sounding Board, Rational,
Logical, Confident,
Discovery

OBJECTIVITY STRENGTH

You are the parent who thinks through your decisions before making a judgment. Whereas many parents make decisions emotionally, you try to identify the reasons for your choices and respond appropriately. When you make a decision regarding your child, you explore all the facts and try to be objective. You weigh the pros and cons, and thoroughly think through your decisions. In the end, you make the right choices because you took the time to think through the consequences. As your child grows, they will seek your help, advice, or guidance with their problems because you are open-minded and will not judge them harshly or let your emotions get in the way.

— Objectivity Parents at Their Best —

Parents strong in the Objectivity strength make reliable decisions, are confident in their choices, and are excellent at getting to the bottom line. They are respected and appreciated for the care and consideration they take when sharing their knowledge and opinions.

▶ **Objectivity Motivators**
security and reduction of uncertainty

▶ **Objectivity Rewards**
good decisions, confidence, information, getting to the bottom of things, low risk, low fear, discovery

▸ **Objectivity Strengths**

confidence, rationality, thoughtfulness, logical reasoning

▸ **Objectivity Struggles**

overly critical, slow decision-
making, anxiety about making the
wrong choice, inconsistent with
rules and consequences

MEET A CHILD'S FIVE ESSENTIAL NEEDS WITH YOUR OBJECTIVITY STRENGTH

▸ **Show Love**

Display an emotionally safe
response to the individual needs
of each child.
Carefully consider your child's
words before speaking.
Remember the details your child
shares.

▸ **Build Trust**

Express rational solutions to
problems and situations.
Weigh family decisions heavily
before implementing them.
Actively listen to better understand your child.

▸ **Establish Structure**

Lead by careful instruction
and consideration.
Logically decide the expectations
of each member of the family.
Explain the reasons behind family
rules and responsibilities.

▸ **Bring Correction**

Share both sides to all situations
and reveal motivations.
Thoroughly explain consequences
for behavior.
Thoughtfully consider the measure of discipline and implement
it firmly.

▸ **Give Hope**

Teach your child that you are not quick to judge or accuse.
Give timely and well-deserved praise.
Provide a clear plan to achieve success.

— Objectivity Parent Action Steps —

Make a ritual of in-depth talks with your child. Discuss anything and everything. Let them use you as a sounding board as they explore and shape their worldviews. Use your Objectivity strength to help them think things through.

Differentiate between crucial decisions and unimportant decisions. Take your time on important decisions. Leverage your full Objectivity strength. But if a decision is inconsequential, treat it as such. There is no need to agonize or stress over making the right decision when the outcome does not matter.

Get your child's opinion. Your child will feel loved and heard when you include them in your decisions. They will see that they have power over their lives. You do not have to agree or act on their opinions. If they are genuinely heard and understood, they will feel validated.

Develop de-stressing habits such as regular meditation, exercise, deep breathing, and journaling. You may find that life and parenting are rushing at you, that you are struggling to find the time to think and that you are not in control. As you engage in these habits, you will feel more in control of your life and more confident in the decisions you are making.

— Parenting Young Children —

If you are the parent of a young child, you analyze their behaviors to identify the reasons for their actions. You take time to process your responses to how your child behaves and rarely let your emotions get the better of you. When you feel frustrated, you pause to identify the reasons you're feeling this way and look for measures to help you stay objective. Your logical approach to parenting gives your young child comfort as you form your parenting strategies through well researched, fact-based tactics—that you will then test to determine effectiveness.

— Parenting Teens —

Your Objectivity strength gives you the ability to remain calm and rational through the season of change and transition associated with the teen years. As your kid ages, you teach them to think before they act. You give them the tools to use to form reasoned, logic-based decisions. Through your strength of Objectivity, you stay in a place of nonjudgment, which builds trust with your kid. They appreciate you for your level-headedness and systematic approach to quality decision-making. Your teen understands your process, and even if they do not always like your conclusions, they respect and appreciate your thoughtfulness.

— Parenting Adults —

If you are the parent of an adult child, your strength of Objectivity is valued by them, since you naturally see both sides of a situation and are not inclined to overreact when presented with a challenging scenario. In this season of life, your grown child seeks you out to think through situations such as career transitions, financial investments, relationship advancements, or personal discord. You are careful to refrain from subjective responses and take time to weigh your reply before giving an answer. You have learned the subtle art of withholding your counsel to allow time for your adult child to take ownership of their decisions and weigh the steps they should take. They will come to you because you are an objective sounding board and they know they can trust your advice.

— Partnering with an Objectivity Parent —

You will always know that your partner has deliberated about the options and is not acting rashly. Your partner wants to make the best choices, to be confident and secure in their decisions.

Your partner probably has issues with uncertainty. Not knowing what is coming or what is the right decision can be very uncomfortable. As such, they want to make careful decisions and try to predict the best outcomes.

When your partner functions in the strength of Objectivity, they apply their rational approach to parenting decisions and surround those decisions with love, warmth, and empathy for their children. They often make secure and safe decisions.

When your partner is struggling with Objectivity, they might feel anxious about their decisions. The thought of making the wrong one can be stressful, even agonizing. You can help your partner by letting them talk through their decisions and counseling together.

— Bring Out the Incredible in Your Objectivity Partner —

Give your partner time to make decisions. Don't ask for one immediately or urgently. Allow them space to process and think. You may want to let your partner talk through their decisions with you. Sometimes, all they will need is a listening ear.

Make decisions before they are imperative. For example, plan how you will deal with developing troubles. Don't wait until you are in the crisis. This won't give your partner enough time to use their Objectivity strength to make the best decision.

Give your partner and your child opportunities to be alone together. Send them out on dates so they can talk. Over time, your child will appreciate this one-on-one experience and start taking advantage of your partner's rational and thoughtful approach. Both partner and child will open up in wonderful ways.

— Understand the Triggers for Your Objectivity Partner —

Don't pressure your partner. Urgent decisions are stressful to them. Ultimatums or added pressure will not speed up their decision—they will just make the process more painful.

Objectivity parents make great decisions, but because their decisions require more work, sometimes they avoid including themselves in the decision-making process—or their partner avoids including them. Do not do this. You will be wasting a truly wonderful strength.

If your partner's stress levels and feelings of frustration or anxiety are long-lasting and are impeding their ability to enjoy life or function, then it may be time to see a professional.

Organizer

Manager, Structure,
Order, Task Creator,
Neat, Coordinates,
Accomplishments, Planner,
Secure, Routines

ORGANIZER STRENGTH

You are the parent who establishes routine and structure for your kids. Whether you are organizing the car pool, setting the chores list for the household, or working with your kids to help them manage their time or money, you likely thrive in a well-organized home. Your kids know they can trust you, and you build on this trust with your consistency and thoroughness. You are the parent who thrives on order and structure, and though you concede that your kids may not have the same organizational needs you do, you see the positive impact of a well-organized home and so work diligently to keep your family on schedule, following the plans you have carefully devised.

— Organizer Parents at Their Best —

Parents strong in the Organizer strength can be clear and concise with their expectations for cleanliness in the home and adherence to organizational principles such as punctuality. They are excellent planners and naturally take the lead in their homes by establishing routine and structure. Organizer parents thrive in effective systems and excel at managing highly efficient household schedules.

▶ Organizer Motivators

structure and accomplishment

▶ Organizer Strengths

ability to plan, direct, organize, lead, and instruct; commanding; finding and creating order; arranging; holding others to high standards; finishing tasks; cleanliness; striving for perfection

▶ Organizer Rewards

cleanliness, knowing exactly where things are, security, consistency, order

▶ Organizer Struggles

rigidity, high-strung tendencies, anxiety, slow or resistant to change

MEET A CHILD'S FIVE ESSENTIAL NEEDS WITH YOUR ORGANIZER STRENGTH

▶ Show Love

Joyfully maintain a sense of order. Spend thoughtful time interacting with your child.
Maintain a safe and clean environment for your children to thrive in.

▶ Build Trust

Communicate consistently to check in with your child.
Engage in your child's activities. Remember special days and events.

▶ Establish Structure

Plan a precise home schedule. Organize the home to function at an optimal level.
Clarify household expectations and standards for cleanliness and order.

▶ Bring Correction

Share the specific steps involved to resolve a problem.
Use cleaning as a form of consequence for discipline. Strictly adhere to implications for your child's actions.

▶ Give Hope

Create an atmosphere of peace with a keen sense of order.
Show the benefits of establishing a stable home environment.
Design a future life for your kid.

— Organizer Parent Action Steps —

As an Organizer, you have a gift for organization, which will help you create sanity and order in the chaos that comes from raising children. Lean into this strength—use it to organize your day, your children's schedules, and your household. Create a system for capturing all the things that you need to do and then set aside time to plan how you will accomplish all those things. Create charts, lists, and calendars, and then stick to them. Establish a regular chore chart or list for your child. Teach them the proper way to do chores. In the beginning, do the chores with them so that they can see the appropriate way to do the tasks. Over time, shift responsibility until the child can adequately do the job by themselves.

Take time every day to schedule things. Collect all the new information or to-do lists from the day. Account for anything that your child brought home from school. Schedule when and where you will accomplish each thing. Be careful not to overbook your child's schedule or your own. Include downtime in the mix so your child can create, explore, and play. You will be a better parent as you allow yourself free time to recharge, rest, and experience joy.

If your schedule allows, get involved in your child's academic or extracurricular activities. Every organization needs someone with your planning and coordinating talent. Getting involved will help you build strong community bonds (crucial social support for your child) and perhaps give you time to interact with them outside your home.

— Parenting Young Children —

You train your child early to not leave their toys around and to pick up after themselves. A tidy room is well organized and efficient—this is a primary lesson you teach. You establish clear expectations for how your child is to treat their possessions and maintain their living space. As your school-age kid is able to take on more household responsibilities, you instill in them a keen sense of the importance of giving their best effort when performing assigned chores. You hold high standards for thoroughness and cleanliness, and this clarity around expectations provides your young child with benchmarks to attain your approval for a job well done.

— Parenting Teens —

You've probably learned to pick your battles in your home. You know what you are willing to let go so your teen can find their personal expression of strength. In this season, you continue to establish routine and structure in your home. With enhanced scheduling techniques, your child appreciates how you ensure every practice, appointment, game, special event, or school function is planned in advance and never missed. You always make sure your teen is prepared, and you work tirelessly to see that no detail is forgotten. They appreciate this about you and have probably grown to respect your need for cleanliness and order in the home.

— Parenting Adults —

Your adult child likely admires the way you organize family holiday gatherings, vacations, and birthday celebrations. Your master calendar and system for informing the family of upcoming events and important dates brings unity to the family. Your child has learned to lean on your Organizer strengths as they enter their child-rearing years and seek to establish a sense of order and predictability in their own homes. You are happy to lend your strengths and find great delight in helping your adult child set up their home. To your family, you are the consistent, steady influence of order and structure. This is a big reason for the trust they have in you.

— Partnering with an Organizer Parent —

Your partner is deeply committed to everything having a place and everything in its place. Order, organization, and cleanliness are vital to their emotional well-being. They will create a home of stability and order that will help your children thrive.

It is important to understand that your partner probably doesn't just like order. They have an intrinsic need for order. They need to create an environment that is structured and organized in order to feel well. Disorder causes stress and tension, and they are compelled to get rid of it. This is why many Organizers say that cleaning brings them joy and is a way of relaxing.

When your partner is in the strength of Organizer, they are training everyone in the family to take part in cleaning and organization. Everyone is reaping the positive benefits of an organized home and life. Your children are doing the things they need to do when they need to do them. They are succeeding in school, at home, and in their hobbies and activities.

When your partner is struggling with their Organizer strength, they might nag you or your child to maintain a cleaner, more organized home/life. They might be angry and frustrated that your home is not up to their standards and feel they are the only one trying to keep your home or life in order. Their need for order starts to create more conflict than peace in the house.

— Bring Out the Incredible in Your Organizer Partner —

Agree on standards, routines, and expectations for your partner, yourself, and your children.

Outline performance expectations and consequences for failing to live up to them. Then support your partner by upholding that agreement yourself and encouraging your children to do so as well.

Make sure that your children are taking part in the cleaning and organization. Give them age-appropriate jobs and then train them to take on more and more responsibility.

— Understand the Triggers for Your Organizer Partner —

Angry cleaning is never a good sign. If your spouse is scrubbing a little too hard, it is time to talk.

Organizers will be frustrated if the family doesn't participate in their home/life organization. Some will mistakenly believe that doing it themselves is easier than fighting with their kids to do it. This is a recipe for burnout and resentment.

Watch for what might be behind the nagging. If your partner is constantly having to pester your child to do their chores, then it is likely that the expectations are not clear enough, the child has not been properly trained to do the expected tasks, or the child is not being held accountable for their work. It may be time to step in and reclarify expectations and consequences.

Sensitivity

Servant, Compassionate,
Support, Listens,
Altruistic, Empathy,
Caring, Helping, Feeling,
Connection

SENSITIVITY STRENGTH

You are a parent who is responsive to the needs of your child and seems to know what they are feeling. You always parent with compassion, especially when your children endure difficult times. When they are sad, you feel their pain and seek to alleviate the hurt with your words and actions. You do not mind rolling up your sleeves and wading into the messes your kids make. You want your child to know you are there for them and will always have their back, no matter what. You seem to "just know" when something is amiss or when your child is not in a great space. This strength provides you with opportunities to demonstrate your care and concern by spending quality time with your kids, getting to really know them and understand them. You take great pleasure in this, and to you, this is one of your primary functions as a parent.

— Sensitivity Parents at Their Best —

Parents strong in the Sensitivity strength empathize, show compassion, and have enhanced emotional awareness. They leverage their Sensitivity strength to build strong bonds of trust with their child and serve as a primary advocate for them. These parents value the connection they have with their child and enjoy being in close proximity and providing personal attention.

▸ **Sensitivity Motivators**

connection and altruism

▸ **Sensitivity Rewards**

bonding, helping, turning negative emotions into positive

▸ **Sensitivity Strengths**

emotional intelligence, compassion, understanding, empathy, emotional awareness

▸ **Sensitivity Struggles**

unfixable situations and people who don't want to change, letting others make mistakes, letting others hurt

MEET A CHILD'S FIVE ESSENTIAL NEEDS WITH YOUR SENSITIVITY STRENGTH

▸ **Show Love**

Prioritize in-depth talks and quality time.
Know when to speak and when to listen.
Outwardly display affection.

▸ **Build Trust**

Demonstrate commitment to discovering your child's intentions before casting judgment.
Provide a neutral and safe space for your child to share freely.
Always be willing to help in times of need.

▸ **Establish Structure**

Help your child understand the deeper reasons for family rules.
Identify your child's emotional triggers and quickly respond to their needs.
Surround your family with people/caretakers who also prioritize care and concern.

▸ **Bring Correction**

Engage in lengthy discussions that lead to a resolution.
Tune into the uniqueness of your child when choosing forms of discipline.
Reinforce your love for your child despite their poor behavior or performance.

▸ **Give Hope**

Be a rock for your child in every storm.
Empathize with every situation and provide words of encouragement and comfort.
Give your child a deep sense of belonging.

— Sensitivity Parent Action Steps —

When your child is having a rough day, let them know that you notice and you are there to talk about it when they're ready. It's okay if it takes a little time for them to open up. Just let them know you are there to love, support, and listen to them.

Nurture your child's compassion. When you notice that other people are struggling, point this out to your child and include them in your efforts to help that person. Ask your child what they think that person is feeling and why that person is feeling that way. Let them create a plan to help that person.

Prevent the meltdown before it happens. You can tell when your child is struggling and on edge. Rather than waiting until they go over that edge, intervene early. Help them take a break from the action, rest, or have some food. Distract them. If they are old enough, talk with them about what they are feeling and why they are feeling that way. Help them identify and manage their emotions early before their feelings become uncontrollable.

— Parenting Young Children —

You have empathy for your young child when they struggle with relationships, or in school, or with their extracurricular activities. You plan talks or special dates with them so you can emphasize how important they are to you. You seem to know exactly what your child is going through, and you ask probing questions without seeming intrusive. Because of your Sensitivity strength, your kid opens up to you about how they feel and about the challenges they face. You are an excellent listener and are genuinely interested in what your child has to say as they share their successes, joys, victories, curiosities, and challenges with you.

— Parenting Teens —

At this stage of parenting, your strength of Sensitivity has made you a trusted advocate for your child. They always know where they stand with you, and you are a source of strength, encouragement, compassion, and moral support. Your teen likely seeks you out to share the victories of their days and excitement for things to come. Equally, when they are challenged or stuck, they seek your listening ear so they can voice their concerns. Even if your teen, in certain seasons, keeps struggles to themselves, you sense when things are off and you identify ways to facilitate safe places for them to open up and share. It is the bond of trust and compassion that binds you and your teen. They know you are in their corner, and even in their darkest times and amid their failures, your steadfast love remains a constant in their lives.

— Parenting Adults —

If you are the parent of an adult child, you have established that you will keep their secrets and always seek first to understand them before needing to be understood. By relating with them in this way, you show how you value their individuality, and they appreciate the way you connect with them by listening first and then asking questions. As such, you are often one of the first phone calls they make when significant life events occur. You delight in this place of honor and always seem to know just what to say to fit the moment you are in with your kid, no matter their age or stage in life.

— Partnering with a Sensitivity Parent —

Your partner has an intuitive sense of the mental and emotional health of your child. They can be excellent at emotionally supporting family members. They always know what your child is feeling and are compassionate enough to help.

Your partner's Sensitivity strength is motivated by true altruism, the selfless desire to help another person. They have a kind heart that wants to help and give. They are naturally selfless and compassionate. Your child will feel that compassion and love, and they will know exactly who to go to when they are struggling.

If your partner is struggling with Sensitivity, it is likely because they feel the pain that others are suffering a little too strongly. They might have a hard time letting your child struggle or fail. They might intervene too early and try to remove all the obstacles in your child's life. Helicopter parenting is born out of a true desire to keep children safe.

It is crucial to counsel together with your partner. You will be able to rely on your partner's Sensitivity strength to understand your child and what they are going through. Occasionally remind your partner that some pain is a good thing and can be an opportunity for growth. Your child can only become a thriving, happy adult if they experience some growing pains.

— Bring Out the Incredible in Your Sensitivity Partner —

Make sure your partner has quality time with your child for in-depth talks.

Encourage your partner to plan fun celebrations of the good things in life.

Encourage them to teach your children how to be aware of, label, and understand their emotions. This will help your kids develop strong emotional awareness and control.

— Understand the Triggers for Your Sensitivity Partner —

Your Sensitivity partner needs time and opportunities to bond, but some families get too busy for authentic connection. You may need to help your partner create those opportunities.

Your child will need to figure out how to learn from their mistakes because you will not always be around. For some parents with Sensitivity, this is hard to accept. Counsel together on how to do this appropriately.

Some Sensitivity parents enable a child because they don't want them to hurt, and this becomes a source of frustration for you both. It is important for them to love the child enough to say no.

Stability

Positive, Balanced, Patient,
Calming, Trustworthy,
Peaceful, Endurance,
Without Worry,
Consistent, Capable

STABILITY STRENGTH

You are a parent who keeps the family calm and stable. You do not let the stress and difficulties of parenting show. You rarely get angry or frustrated, and in those rare times when you do, you effectively deal with your negative emotions. Your Stability strength brings balance and calmness to your home. No matter what stresses exist outside of the house, your kid knows that because of you, their homelife has a sure foundation. You are not bothered by your child's faults and failures; to you, these are part of the learning process. As your kid grows and matures, you continue to be fascinated by them and so can overcome the pull to frustration when your expectations are not met and your child falls short.

— Stability Parents at Their Best —

Parents strong in the Stability strength are not easily angered and do not often succumb to fear or anxiety. They are calm in life's storms and maintain composure when faced with difficult circumstances. Their homes are peaceful, their demeanor is steady, and they are the rock their families depend on.

▶ Stability Motivators

peace and calm

▶ Stability Strengths

keeping calm; not prone to anxiety, worry, anger, fear, frustration, jealousy, guilt, depression, discouragement, or loneliness; handling adversity; enduring difficult situations

▶ Stability Rewards

calm household, lack of stress, lack of anxiety, positive emotions

▶ Stability Struggles

lack of understanding when and why a child reacts emotionally, less attention to errors, minimization of issues

---

MEET A CHILD'S FIVE ESSENTIAL NEEDS WITH YOUR STABILITY STRENGTH

▶ Show Love

Maintain an attitude of genuine interest in your child.
Stay involved with your child's extracurricular activities.
Be a consistent source of encouragement to your child.

▶ Establish Structure

Set the consequences for poor behaviors in advance. Ask for peace and quiet in the home.
Teach your child to follow your example.

▶ Give Hope

Genuinely display a joyful attitude despite life's trials.
Encourage your child to see the bright side of things.
Listen without judgment.

▶ Build Trust

Maintain composure and do not overreact to stressful situations.
Stand by your word with your child.
Be consistent with responses in all circumstances.

▶ Bring Correction

Provide patient instruction when an explanation of expectations is needed.
Follow through with the consequences given.
Maintain a stable demeanor in difficult situations and when speaking.

— Stability Parent Action Steps —

When your child acts up, step up. Use your Stability strength to calm and defuse the situation. With patience, teach your child the consequences of their negative behaviors, and then help them see and understand the implications of other positive actions.

Train your child to solve their problems rather than dwell on them. Help them figure out a variety of ways to deal with a particular challenge so they see the alternatives, even if they don't put them to use in that situation. Be careful that you don't solve the problem for them.

Teach your child how to reframe their challenges. Acknowledge their negative emotions, then help them come up with the positives of the situation.

Some incredible parents teach their children that when they are down about something, they should say, "This is awesome because…" and come up with a reason that the situation is incredible. However, be careful not to minimize or disregard your children's emotional experiences. While perception is not reality, it sure feels like it is. When we trivialize problems, we don't make them go away. We just make our children feel stupid for having the problem at all. Now they have the problem *and* they feel silly. Rather than minimize, express compassion and empathy. Help them reframe without diminishing the significance of a challenge or their feelings about it.

— Parenting Young Children —

If you are the parent of a young child, your Stability strength shines through as you make your way through the infant and toddler years with ease and grace. You understand, innately, that children will be children and therefore will act in a manner consistent with a child's age and stage. This perspective helps you stay calm during challenging circumstances such as when the child has tantrums, whines, and acts out in a manner inconsistent with your expectations. As your kid reaches school age, your strength of Stability shows up in the mood and tone you set for your home. To your child, you always seem to be in a good mood, and they love to tell you about their day, what they learned, and their various adventures.

— Parenting Teens —

Your strength of Stability is tested by the independence and individuality of your teen, yet you are known by them as the parent who is seldom angry with them and almost never responds to their behavior with a raised voice. When it comes time to bring correction regarding unmet expectations or rule violations, you can be counted on to do so with measured speech and carefully crafted words about expected behavior in the future. Because of this calm demeanor, your teen or adolescent reaches out to you during their darkest times or after their most serious accidents or incidents. They enjoy your relaxed nature and your easygoing personality. Your teen, and likely their friends, view you as easy to get along with because you represent a safe and secure person whom they can rely on.

— Parenting Adults —

In your adult child's life, you are a source of calming influence when stress and strife are present. Because you are the "same parent" each time a conversation occurs, not too upbeat nor too cynical, your adult child enjoys your soothing presence and your predictability in their grown-up life and its subsequent joys and sorrows. In crisis, your Stability strength shows up mightily. This probably explains why your adult kid seeks you out if they encounter a situation beyond their experience or one that is particularly distressing.

— Partnering with a Stability Parent —

Your partner is slow to anger and quick to make peace. They have a unique ability to withstand situations that would make other people lose their tempers. Your partner rarely feels the negative side of the emotional spectrum, which is why they are such a calming presence in your home.

Your partner's emotional stability is rooted in their natural strength of forbearance. It takes a lot to make them feel angry, sad, frustrated, or depressed. They feel these emotions just like everyone else; they just don't give in to them as easily.

When your partner is in the strength of Stability, they are a peacemaker in your home. They are the calming presence and voice that defuses conflict and stress. They can help you and your kids step back, breathe, and reset when you start to feel frustrated, angry, or anxious.

Sometimes, your partner might unintentionally minimize your feelings or reactions. Since it is not a big deal to them, they assume that it shouldn't be a big deal to others. This attitude can make you feel disrespected and lead to resentment. When this occurs, you and your partner will need to work together and intentionally strive for understanding.

At times, your partner might also minimize your child's problematic behaviors. They are so forbearing that they allow issues to go on for too long before they are addressed. You can bring out the best in your partner by establishing behavioral expectations for your child together. Agree on what is or is not appropriate behavior, and then create a united, consistent front.

— Bring Out the Incredible in Your Stability Partner —

Give in to their calming influence. They will try to defuse tense situations. People in strong relationships will allow themselves to be calmed by their partners.

Counsel with your partner before making an emotional decision. Their Stability strength will help you make the right decision, not just an emotional one.

Encourage them to lean into their Stability strength in discipline conversations. Those can be intense and frustrating experiences. If they use their Stability strength throughout the conversation, it will be a more positive and productive experience for everyone involved.

— Understand the Triggers for Your Stability Partner —

Sometimes, in their attempts to restore peace, your partner might avoid conflict or completely shut down a conversation by ignoring you or your children. The stonewalling is not a healthy response and should be replaced with constructive conversations.

Your partner is motivated by peace and harmony, and they will struggle in situations that produce frequent or intense negative emotions.

Tenderness

Happy, Gentle, Playful,
Grateful, Loving, Valued,
Nurturing, Attentive,
Warm, Sacrificial

TENDERNESS STRENGTH

You are the parent who always tries to do nice things for your child and make them feel special and loved. You play with them, cheer them up, celebrate their victories, and get excited with them. You model kindness by going out of your way to help others in need. You are always available to help a friend or neighbor or even a stranger. Your child sees this and knows you are never too busy to help them, and they never doubt your love. You will drop what you are doing when your kid looks to you for aid or assurance. Your Tenderness strength is reflected in your kindness and overt displays of love and affection.

— Tenderness Parents at Their Best —

Parents strong in the Tenderness strength are never hesitant to show love to their children and display it with practical acts of service and thoughtful gestures. They generally have warm personalities and enjoy serving their children above their own interests.

▶ **Tenderness Motivators**
love and affection

▶ **Tenderness Rewards**
making someone feel special, expressions of gratitude, hugs, kisses, thoughtful cards, cuddles, words of affirmation, attachment

▶ Tenderness Strengths

expressions of love, warm personality, thoughtful gestures, willingness to sacrifice

▶ Tenderness Struggles

jealousy, loneliness, codependence, smothering, sacrificing too much, difficulty with conflict and negative emotions

MEET A CHILD'S FIVE ESSENTIAL NEEDS WITH YOUR TENDERNESS STRENGTH

▶ Show Love

Give individualized attention to each child.
Show love for your child through outward displays of affection.
Be a student of your child's love language and provide love in the unique way your child receives.

▶ Build Trust

Show concern by recognizing when your kid needs assistance.
Don't judge your child or compare them to others.
Sacrifice personal desires for the benefit of your child.

▶ Establish Structure

Create and adhere to healthy routines in the home.
Consistently express daily positive affirmations to your child.
Encourage each member of the household to serve others.

▶ Bring Correction

Gently explain the consequences for negative actions.
Share consistent affirming words when disciplining.
Relate to a child's failings and disobedience and tell stories to connect with them.

▶ Give Hope

Provide your child with a deep sense of belonging as a member of the family.
Eagerly share with your child the person you see them becoming as they grow up.
Show your child unconditional love despite their outward behavior.

— Tenderness Parent Action Steps —

Learn your child's love language. What are their primary and secondary ways of feeling loved? Establish a habit of showing them love in their language.

Teach your child how to show love and be kind by including them in the positive things you do. You probably do something kind for someone almost every day—sending a get-well card to a friend, leaving a kind note for your spouse, offering to babysit for a sick parent, volunteering at school, and so on. Let your child take part in your service. Give them a taste of how wonderful it feels to serve. They will, over time, learn to love it, and they will start doing it at home, filling your household with love and kindness.

Connect with your loved ones every single day. It is not enough to say "I love you" or to give hugs if you aren't also connecting. Even if it is only 30 seconds, take time every day to truly show appreciation and love.

— Parenting Young Children —

If you are the parent of a young child, you go out of your way to shower them with loving acts of service and thoughtful displays of love and affection. You love to hug your kids and sit with them for snuggle time. Your thoughtfulness is very intentional and never one-size-fits-all. You consider the uniqueness of your child and seek to demonstrate your love by going on outings or doing activities that they will treasure. As your child matures, you enjoy involvement in their school and extracurricular activities. Doing beautiful things for your kids brings you great satisfaction. When they smile, you smile.

— Parenting Teens —

When parenting a teen or adolescent, your strength can be seen in the way you get as excited for their good fortunes as you do your own. Bringing delight to your teen is great fun. You genuinely enjoy being with them and doing things with them that they enjoy or that you can introduce them to. Taking trips to new places, trying new food, or making memories and discoveries close to home are acts of joy for you. When your teen isn't feeling or doing well, they lean on your strength of Tenderness to care for them and check in on them. Because you have a reputation for being willing to help your kid with their projects, problems, and people issues, they trust your considerate nature and thoughtfulness.

— Parenting Adults —

Your strength of Tenderness is on display when you lend a helping hand to your adult child during transitions like starting college, a career, and a family. You are known as your child's most stalwart supporter and a source of strength, encouragement, and comfort. You make time to regularly communicate, and you never place conditions on your displays of love and generosity by using manipulation tactics to get their attention. You delight in showing kindness to your child in practical ways. Therefore, if they encounter financial challenges, relational discord, health issues, or life stresses, you make it known that you are there to be a source of help and support in any and all circumstances. If you have grandchildren, you love to play a supportive role in their development as well.

— Partnering with a Tenderness Parent —

Your partner is overflowing with love and affection, especially toward your children. They go above and beyond to make your children happy. To them, your children feeling happy is one of their primary reasons for living.

Your partner's Tenderness strength carries with it an intense need to love and be loved in return. Expressing love and having that love reciprocated makes them feel fulfilled. This is why they so frequently express their affection.

When your partner is in the strength of Tenderness, they serve everyone in the home and do the little things to make each person happy. They balance their service with self-care and understand that others don't express love as frequently or in the same ways that they do. They allow others to have space and love them on their terms.

If your partner is struggling with Tenderness, they may be wearing themselves out in service of their family. Some Tenderness parents might emotionally "overinvest" in children and create unhealthy dependencies. You can help your Tenderness partner by assisting them in developing other positive relationships and outside hobbies.

— Bring Out the Incredible in Your Tenderness Partner —

Help them establish daily routines with your child that allow them to connect with and show love. Bedtime routines are a favorite of many Tenderness parents.

Encourage playtime between your partner and your child. It's healthy for both of them.

Help your partner learn your child's love language. Your partner has their own language, but to help your child feel loved, your partner will need to use your child's love language.

— Understand the Triggers for Your Tenderness Partner —

In the quest to be loved, your partner might give in to your children and not hold them accountable to your expectations. Avoid the cycle of permissive parenting by staying on the same page with your partner about the priorities you have set together.

Unbalanced work and life schedules are a source of frustration for your Tenderness partner. It hurts them tremendously if they miss out on spending time with and being there for your child because of work, yet sometimes your partner will need you to remind them of this priority so they can keep these areas of life organized and balanced.

As your children grow, they will start spending more time outside the home. For some Tenderness parents, this is a very hard transition, and they can experience unhealthy jealousy.

Trainer

Authority, Control,
Boundaries, Purposeful
Rules, Guides, Teacher,
Leads, Expectations,
Order, Consistent

TRAINER STRENGTH

You are the parent who brings order to your home by making sure you clearly define the expectations for your child. You also communicate your feelings of approval or disapproval so your kid always knows where they stand. You expect compliance and look for commitment from your kids to do as they're told. Your Trainer strength establishes the rules and boundaries that are in place so that each member of your household is considerate toward one another. Your child respects you and understands that your discipline is born of your deep love for them and your desire to see them succeed in life.

— Trainer Parents at Their Best —

Parents strong in the Trainer strength excel at establishing codes of behavior and making sure every member of the household knows what is expected of them. They are strong at providing explicit rules of engagement and incentives for adherence to the social expectations of the family. Their kids respect them and trust them because they always know where they stand with them.

▶ **Trainer Motivators**
order and control

▶ **Trainer Rewards**
obedience, regulation, direction, authority

▶ Trainer Strengths

training people to obey rules, establishing a code of behavior, creating consistent behavior, setting expectations

▶ Trainer Struggles

controlling and strict, punitive or unforgiving, heavily reliant on authority, perceived as rude, triggered by disrespect

MEET A CHILD'S FIVE ESSENTIAL NEEDS WITH YOUR TRAINER STRENGTH

▶ Show Love

Engage with your child in their activities.

Provide positive reinforcement and encouragement for your child. Clearly define expectations and requirements for adherence to standards and consequences for noncompliance.

▶ Establish Structure

Set explicit expectations for behavior and ensure they are understood.

Create a controlled environment in which your child will flourish. Implement and teach good habits.

▶ Build Trust

Demonstrate the behavior expected of your child. Support your child in all activities with hands-on or sideline coaching. Motivate and inspire your kid with words of affirmation.

▶ Bring Correction

Explain your core values in a consistent manner so they cannot be misinterpreted or misunderstood. Enforce consequences when expectations are unmet or values are not followed. Provide constructive feedback to teach your kid to make better choices.

▶ Give Hope

Assure your child of their worth and capabilities. Make sure your child knows what to expect. Vigorously support your child in their academic or extracurricular endeavors.

— Trainer Parent Action Steps —

Establish rules ahead of time, then allow your child the freedom to operate within those rules. Your child may not do things the same way that you would or even the way that you would like them to, but if they are not breaking the rules, they need to be given the freedom to choose how to follow them. Then you must be consistent in enforcing those rules.

Agree with your partner on the consequences for inappropriate behavior ahead of time. It is essential that your discipline is not capricious, fits the inappropriate behavior, and is acceptable to your spouse. If everyone, including your child, knows what the consequences are ahead of time, your crucial conversation with your child about what transpired can shift from "You did this bad thing. Here is your punishment" to "You know what the consequences are. Now let's talk about what you could have done differently."

Discuss the reasons for your household rules with your children often. Your children will fight you if they feel that your standards are arbitrary or harmful to them. However, if your children understand why the rules are essential to the happiness and safety of themselves and others, then they can start to embrace them instead. Your kids will see the underlying principles and moral code that you are trying to teach them and will begin generalizing those principles into other aspects of their lives.

Focus most of your attention on what your child is doing right. Praise them and reinforce them whenever you see them acting appropriately and following the rules. You can shape your child's behaviors much faster by reinforcing the positive than by punishing the negative.

— Parenting Young Children —

You instill in your young child the importance of finishing what they start and following through on their commitments. It is important to you that your kid be a person of their word and a respectable member of their schools, sports teams, and clubs. You establish standards of behavior for your child in public places and within the homes of family and friends. Respecting authority and adults in their life is a lesson you reinforce. Your goal is to make your expectations crystal clear for your kid and hold them accountable for their actions. You provide a standard to help them understand how to best measure up to the expectations by giving examples of proper behavior and gently instructing them when they miss the mark. When your child fails to be honest, you don't hold it over their head. Instead, you reestablish your expectations.

— Parenting Teens —

For your teen, you create clear, unambiguous expectations and subsequent consequences for misbehavior. In fact, it becomes a point of emphasis because as your teen looks to gain autonomy, their decisions become more consequential. During this season, you are careful to apply the correct measures to match the age, stage, and maturity of your teen. You do not tolerate dishonesty. Your goal is to prepare them to become an adult who is ready and willing to be responsible for their own actions and accountable for the successes and failures in their life. You spend time with your teen or adolescent, making sure they are engaged in growing and maturing. You loosen the reins as they demonstrate a firm grasp on mature adult concepts. You take great delight in helping your teen embody the principles you have sought to instill in them from a young age.

— Parenting Adults —

If you are the parent of an adult child, your Trainer strength is present to offer perspective on their choices and consequences—when requested to share. You are happy to let their life play out, acting as a source of strength and reinforcement, reminding them of the values and principles relevant to your family. During this season of life, you enjoy sharing with your adult kid the ways they make you proud, reminding them of the successes and victories you have observed throughout their life. When asked, you are happy to help them establish expectations for their own family.

— Partnering with a Trainer Parent —

Your partner has a unique ability to create structure and order in your home. They excel in creating and enforcing rules and expectations for behavior. They often parent with authority and create stability in the home.

Your partner has a strong desire to control and regulate your child's behavior in order to increase their chance of leading a successful and productive life. They want to create boundaries for your children so that your kids can safely thrive. When your partner is in the strength of Trainer, they discipline and enforce structure with five parts reinforcement and one part correction. They focus more on developing the right behavior than punishing the wrong kind.

When your partner is facing Trainer struggles, they might attempt to overcontrol your child's behavior. They might engage in a spiral of fighting, punishment, more fighting, more severe punishment, and so on.

To bring out the best in your partner, help them focus on

"catching" your child doing the right things. Use positive reinforcement of proper behavior as the primary training tool. And together, agree on a code of conduct that you can consistently enforce.

— Bring Out the Incredible in Your Trainer Partner —

Regularly talk with your spouse about all the things that your child is doing right. Together, create a family culture of appreciation and respect for one another.

Counsel together on the code of conduct for your family. Agree on the consequences for obedience and disobedience.

Praise your partner when you see their Trainer talent bringing out the best in your child. Appreciate their talent in action.

— Understand the Triggers for Your Trainer Partner —

The inconsistent enforcement of rules will lead to frustration and potential arguments. Children often test boundaries, and if the boundaries are constantly moving, they will react against what they regard as unfairness.

Discipline should always have the goal of helping children learn to make amends for their poor choices as well as how to make better choices in the future. If there is overly harsh punishment, children can't get past the injustice and actually learn the lesson.

If it seems like your Trainer partner is operating from a place of conditional love, it is important to discuss how vital it is for a child to feel unconditional love from each parent, even during the enforcement of rules. Love, kindness, and warmth should never be contingent on how your child behaves.

Zest

Passionate, Fun,
Enthusiastic, Active,
Motivating, Energetic,
Celebrates, Laughter,
Relational, Adventurous

ZEST STRENGTH

You are the parent who lives for each new day with passion and enthusiasm. You derive energy from and, with your strength of Zest, give your very best effort to parenting, which is one of the great joys of your life. Your child trusts you and knows you are engaged in their life, never content to sit on the sidelines. Because parenting energizes you, you are always looking ahead with great anticipation toward the future in store for your child. You enjoy each new adventure you partake in with your kid, and they love your Zest for life. You never give half-hearted effort to your parenting and continuously look for ways to grow and learn from your mistakes. To you, making a mistake is the highest form of learning. You don't linger long in disappointment or discouragement after a setback. You recover quickly and move forward with purpose, eager to see your child become all they were made to be.

— Zest Parents at Their Best —

Parents strong in Zest are playful, fun, and love to laugh. Zest parents enjoy life and especially delight in being a parent. The adventure of parenting is an opportunity to experience life through the eyes of their child, and this is a wonderful experience. They are always learning and growing. They don't take themselves too seriously and, as such, are highly relatable. Parents strong on Zest are often friends with their adult kids.

▶ **Zest Motivators**

pleasure and excitement

▶ **Zest Strengths**

optimism, playfulness, activeness, engagement, energy, prone to positive emotions, open to change

▶ **Zest Rewards**

new adventures, novelty, friendship, laughter, fun, joy

▶ **Zest Struggles**

flighty and inconsistent, easily bored, wrestles with routines

MEET A CHILD'S FIVE ESSENTIAL NEEDS WITH YOUR ZEST STRENGTH

▶ **Show Love**

Engage enthusiastically with your child.
Celebrate big and small moments.
Dote on your child with excess and take great pride in their accomplishments.

▶ **Establish Structure**

Make daily routines fun.
Cocreate a culture of your home that everyone buys into.
Set up rewards and celebrations for accomplishing tasks and weekly assignments.

▶ **Give Hope**

Celebrate your unique child and instill a strong sense of value.
Be excited about the future and rejoice in the success your child will enjoy.
Believe in the best future for your child in all circumstances.

▶ **Build Trust**

Focus on being available for frequent playful interactions with your child.
Ask questions of your child to learn their likes and dislikes.
Create special moments with your kid that reinforce their value and importance.

▶ **Bring Correction**

Give instructions with a positive outlook.
Explain the consequences for actions and then express an eagerness to get back to more enjoyable things.
Look to the future and don't dwell on the past.

— Zest Parent Action Steps —

Share your wonder of the world with your child. Whenever you feel elevation, gratitude, love, or excitement, include your child in this experience. Share with them what you're feeling and help them savor the moment with you.

Include your child in your adventures and activities. At first, it may feel like you're lugging your child around and that they're holding you back from truly enjoying your experience. However, over time, they will become a more skilled and more active participant. You will soon develop shared hobbies and interests. Your relationship will grow deeper.

Add some spice and novelty to your routines. You are creative and spontaneous. Use that to your advantage in parenting. Mix up the methods. You don't have to do anything significant, because even slight changes can create joy and excitement to your child. For example, bust out the bubbles for bath time. Add food coloring to your pancake batter. Instead of coming straight home from school, stop by the playground for 10 minutes. Add happy things to your lives, such as water balloons, picnics, breakfast for dinner, random game nights, and on and on.

Create a community for your kid. Children need a variety of strong relationships with children and adults. They thrive when there is a wider group of people who care for them. You can join an existing community like a church, hobby club, school, or sports groups. You can also create your own by bonding with the neighborhood families.

Take time every day to play with your child. Have a tea party. Play with Legos. Go to the park and be the lava monster. Play soccer. Dress up. Have a backyard campout. You are at your best when you are enjoying spending time with your child. But with all the demands on parents and families today, you must be intentional about taking that time every day.

— Parenting Young Children —

A young child sees your enthusiasm and knows that you love being a parent. You make it your ambition to deeply know your kids and engage them in the grand adventure of life. You enjoy volunteering for and attending their activities and endeavors. Your gift of hospitality likely leads you to host various events and gatherings that are fun for everyone.

— Parenting Teens —

Your teen may enjoy hosting gatherings with their friends at your home because you provide a fun and safe place to be. Your involvement intensifies in the teen years, as you enjoy the time you have with your kids in the house. At every stage of your child's life, you take time to know your child's friends and the parents too.

— Parenting Adults —

If you are the parent of an adult child, you are likely friends with them and genuinely enjoy spending time with them traveling, enjoying holiday gatherings, or chatting about how life is going and what they are up to. Your strength of Zest is appreciated by your adult child. They have come to rely on your upbeat attitude, true and transparent love for life, and genuine interest in their success.

— Partnering with a Zest Parent —

Your partner brings fun into parenting. They help your child discover the joy and little pleasures in life. They fill your home with laughter, stories, fun, and excitement. They create a home of play. They probably plan lots of family activities, new adventures, and playdates, and they fill up your child's social and activity calendar.

When your partner is in the strength of Zest, they aren't just saving the fun and adventure for holidays; they are creating adventure in everyday life. They are bringing the family together to laugh, love, and enjoy one another. They are having fun being a parent.

Some Zest parents can struggle with the monotony of parenting. Parenting is full of routines. Most days look much like the last. For some Zest parents, this can be boring and make them feel unengaged. These Zest parents may need to be encouraged to use their strength to bring joy into chores, homework, shopping, and all the other things that a parent needs to do.

Another struggle of some Zest parents is the tendency to put off responsibilities in the home or life in favor of fun. They can inadvertently teach your child that work is unpleasant and should be avoided. Bring out the best in your partner by encouraging them not to avoid work but to make it fun for everyone.

— Bring Out the Incredible in Your Zest Partner —

Ask your partner to plan the next family vacation. Let them make it fun and exciting.

Have friends over for the kids and your partner. Social relationships are often little happy pills for parents with Zest.

Avoid the evening TV trap. Your partner needs fun. TV is an easy way to be entertained, but to bring out the best in your partner, you will want to let them create fun evening activities for you and the family.

— Understand the Triggers for Your Zest Partner —

If your partner is putting off their work and responsibilities, their Zest strength is probably not getting fed. Help them by having real fun, not just relaxation.

Zest parents can get bored with routine. Too much consistency can cause your partner to feel disengaged. Help them spice up their routine and find things to get excited about.

Maximize Your Super Six Incredible Parent Strengths
Connect with a Certified Incredible Parent Master Coach

William Chaney—coachchaney@outlook.com

Rhonda Knight-Boyle—rhonda.boyle@gmail.com

Madlin Mangrum—coach@madlinmangrum.com (Español)

Sheena Fleener—sheena.fleener@gmail.com

MaLinda Perry— malinda.j.perry@gmail.com

Jay and Faith Kenton—jay.kenton@gmail.com (说话)

Cynthia Stewart—cynthia@evermoreservices.com

Gloria Gonzalez—gloriakelleygonzalez@icloud.com

Anita McGee—mcgeemarket@gmail.com

Guillaume Lepenher—guillaume.lepenher@gmail.com (Français)

Ed Miller—the3pathways@gmail.com

Polly Tonti—ptonti15@outlook.com

For media requests or speaking engagements,
connect with Analyn and Brandon at
www.AnalynBrandon.com